weebee Series One (Books 1 – 8) Complete Resource Book

CROSSBRIDGE BOOKS

Published by:

Crossbridge Books
Worcester

© R M Price-Mohr 2020

All rights reserved. No part of this publication may be reproduced, stored in a retrieval system or transmitted in any form or by any means – electronic, mechanical, recording or otherwise – without prior permission of the copyright owner.

Permission is given to photocopy the resource pages.

ISBN 978-1-913946-08-1

weebee Series One Resource Book (Books 1 – 8)

This book contains photocopy-able pages with games and activities designed to support the learning of vocabulary and targeted phonic sounds used in the weebee series one (Books 1 – 8).

A list of the new vocabulary introduced with each book along with the story text is provided for all books. Lists of the target phonic sounds and high frequency words are also included for each book. The phonic sounds largely follow the 'Letters and Sounds' phonic phases. The high frequency words are from the 100 most common words in written English that comprise, on average, one half of all reading materials.

A handbook and other resources can be downloaded free of charge from the website:

https://crossbridgeeducational.com/

weebee Series 1 (Books 1-8) Complete Resource Book

Contents:	Page

Book 1 (Grog) Word list, targeted phonics, high frequency words and text	4
Bingo	6
Dominoes	16
Phonics sheet (_an)	24
Book 2 (Pip) Word list, targeted phonics, high frequency words and text	26
Fishing Lotto	28
Memory	38
Phonics sheet (_in)	42
Book 3 (Tod) Word list, targeted phonics, high frequency words and text	44
Bingo	46
Dominoes	56
Phonics sheet (_ed)	64
Octologo	66
Book 4 (Mop) Word list, targeted phonics, high frequency words and text	78
Fishing Lotto	80
Memory	88
Happy Word Families	92
Phonics sheet (_ow)	98
Octologo	100
Book 5 (Jig) Word list, targeted phonics, high frequency words and text	102
Bingo	104
Dominoes	114
Happy Word Families	126
Phonics sheet (_ip)	132
Octologo	134
Book 6 (Zon) Word list, targeted phonics, high frequency words and text	136
Fishing Lotto	138
Memory	146
Happy Word Families	150
Phonics sheet (_it)	156
Octologo	158
Book 7 (Flup) Word list, targeted phonics, high frequency words and text	160
Bingo	162
Dominoes	172
Happy Word Families	184
Phonics sheet (_og)	190
Octologo	192
Book 8 (Saff) Word list, targeted phonics, high frequency words and text	194
Fishing Lotto	196
Memory	204
Happy Word Families	208
Phonics sheet (_nk)	214
Octologo	216
Pupil Tracking Sheet	218

Grog 1

Words list:

green	a	nest	can
he	pond	weebee	sleep
happy	tree	this	at
and	look	is	asleep
his	in	Grog	red

Targeted phonics:

_ee_
_oo_
_nd
gr_
_st
_an

High frequency words:

a
he
and
in
is
at

Text:

1. a pond
2. a tree
3. look in
4. a nest
5. a weebee
6. this is Grog
7. Grog is green and his nest is red and green
8. he is happy in his nest
9. Grog can sleep in his nest
10. look at Grog asleep in his red and green nest

weebee Series 1 (Books 1-8) Complete Resource Book

at		nest
	pond	tree
can	green	
his		sleep
	red	weebee
in	look	

Book 1 Bingo sheet 1

and		this
	pond	tree
can	Grog	
red		sleep
	at	weebee
	look	

Book 1 Bingo sheet 2

weebee Series 1 (Books 1-8) Complete Resource Book

he		nest
	pond	this
and	happy	
his		sleep
	at	weebee
is	Grog	

Book 1 Bingo sheet 3

at		nest
	pond	this
can	green	
his		Grog
	is	happy
and	he	

Book 1 Bingo sheet 4

weebee Series 1 (Books 1-8) Complete Resource Book

at	and	nest
sleep	pond	this
can	green	tree
his	look	Grog
red	is	happy
in	he	weebee

Book 1 Bingo word sheet

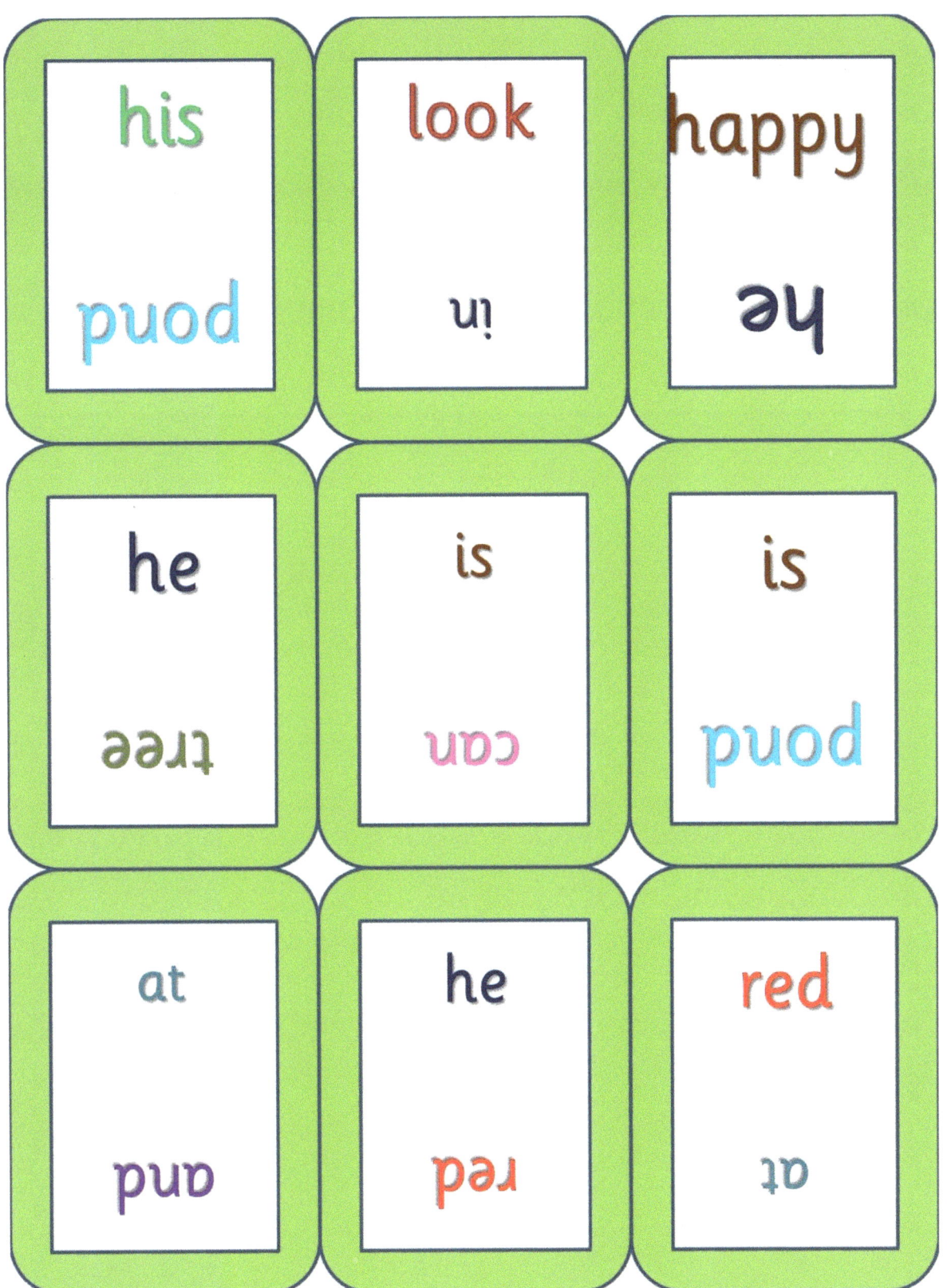

Book 1 Dominoes sheet 1

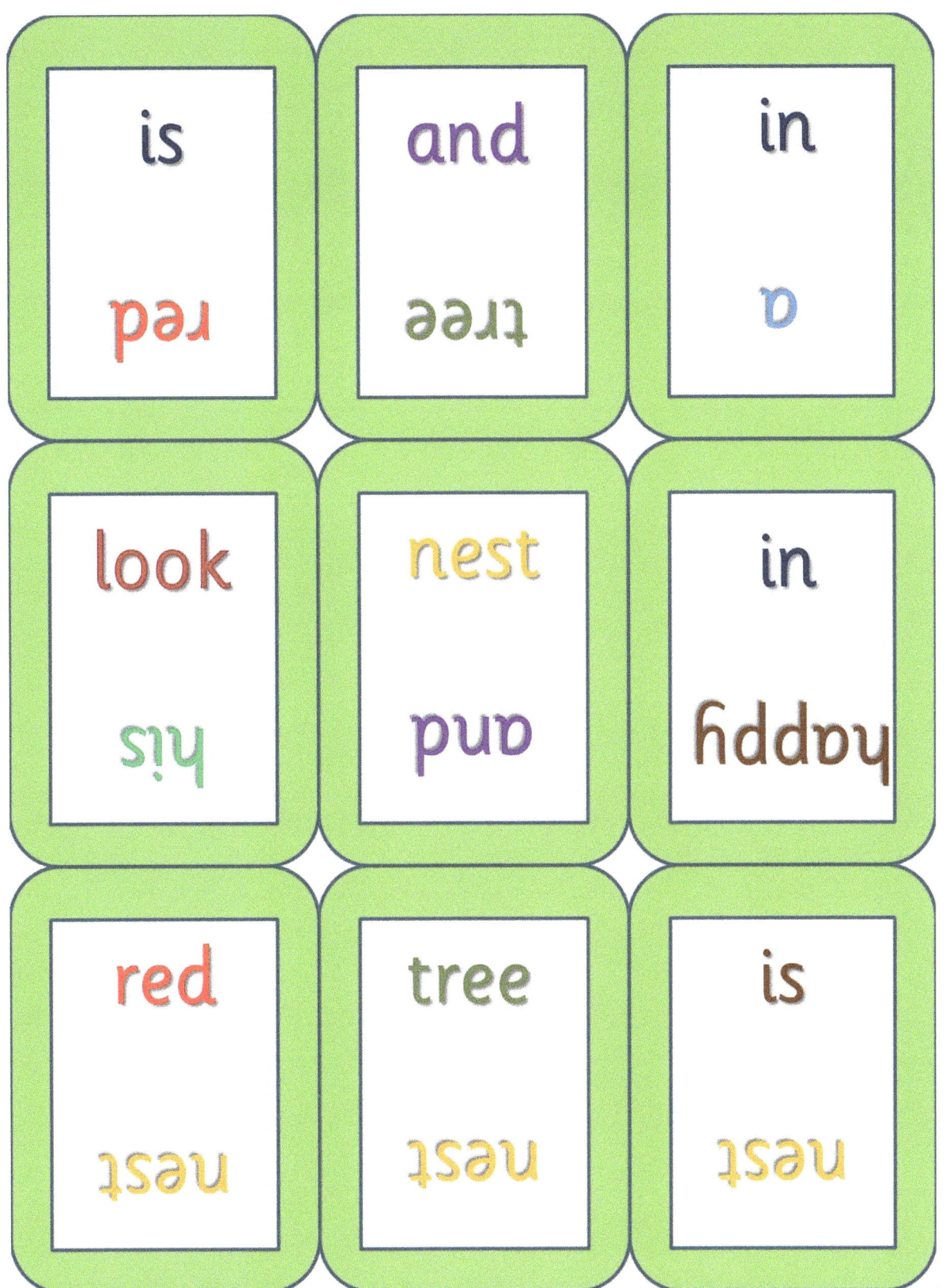

Book 1 Dominoes sheet 2

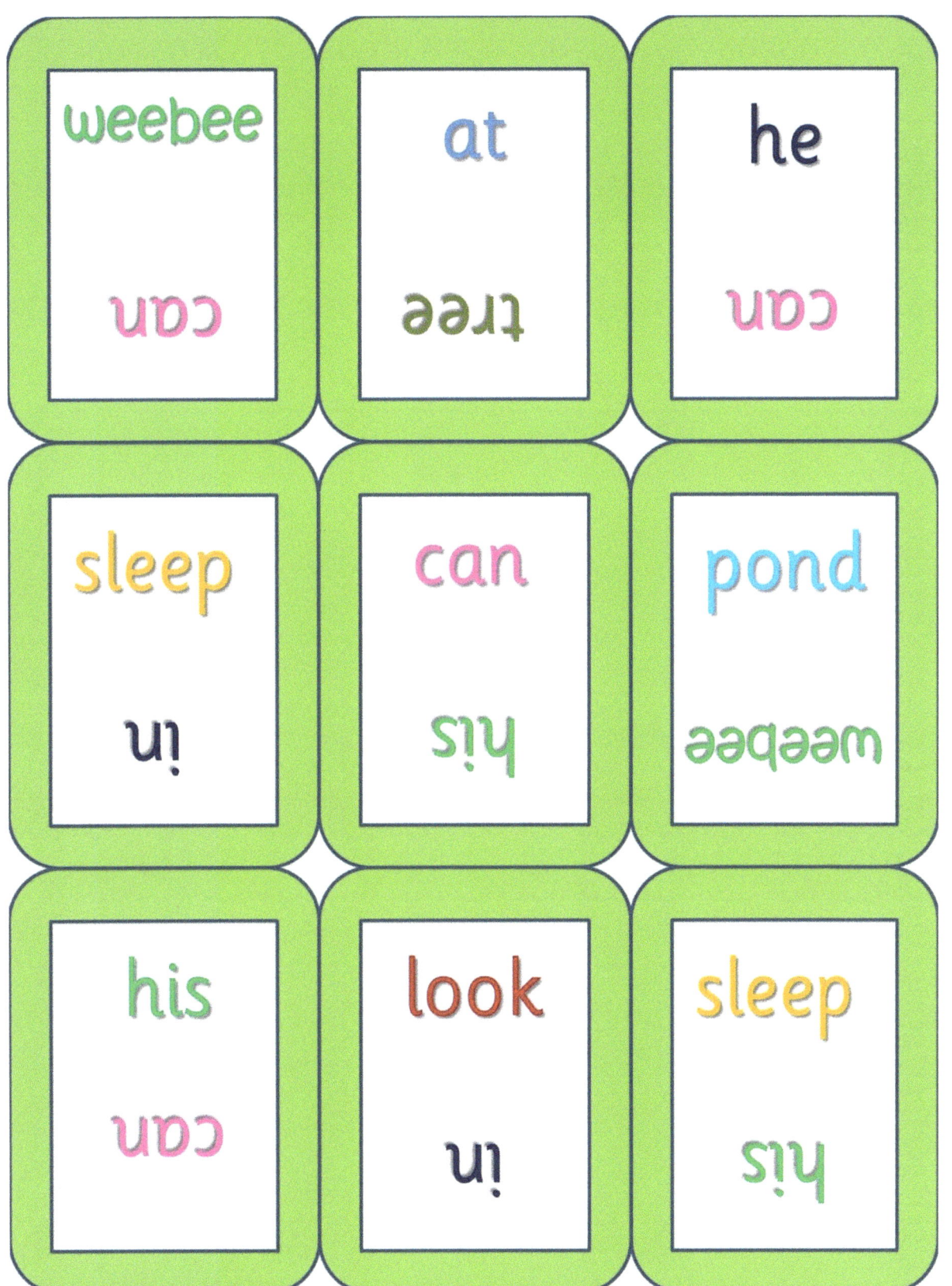

Book 1 Dominoes sheet 3

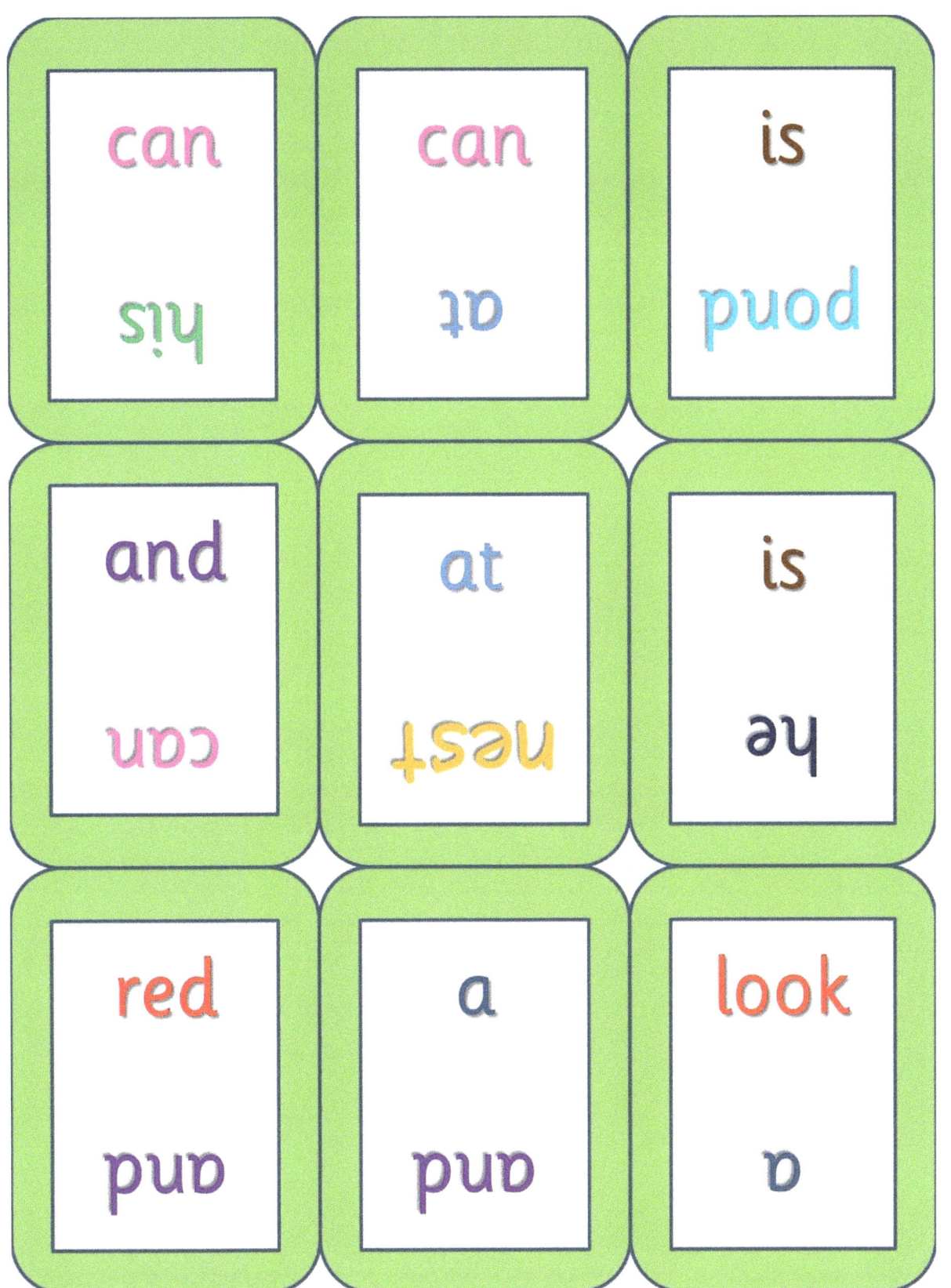

Book 1 Dominoes sheet 4

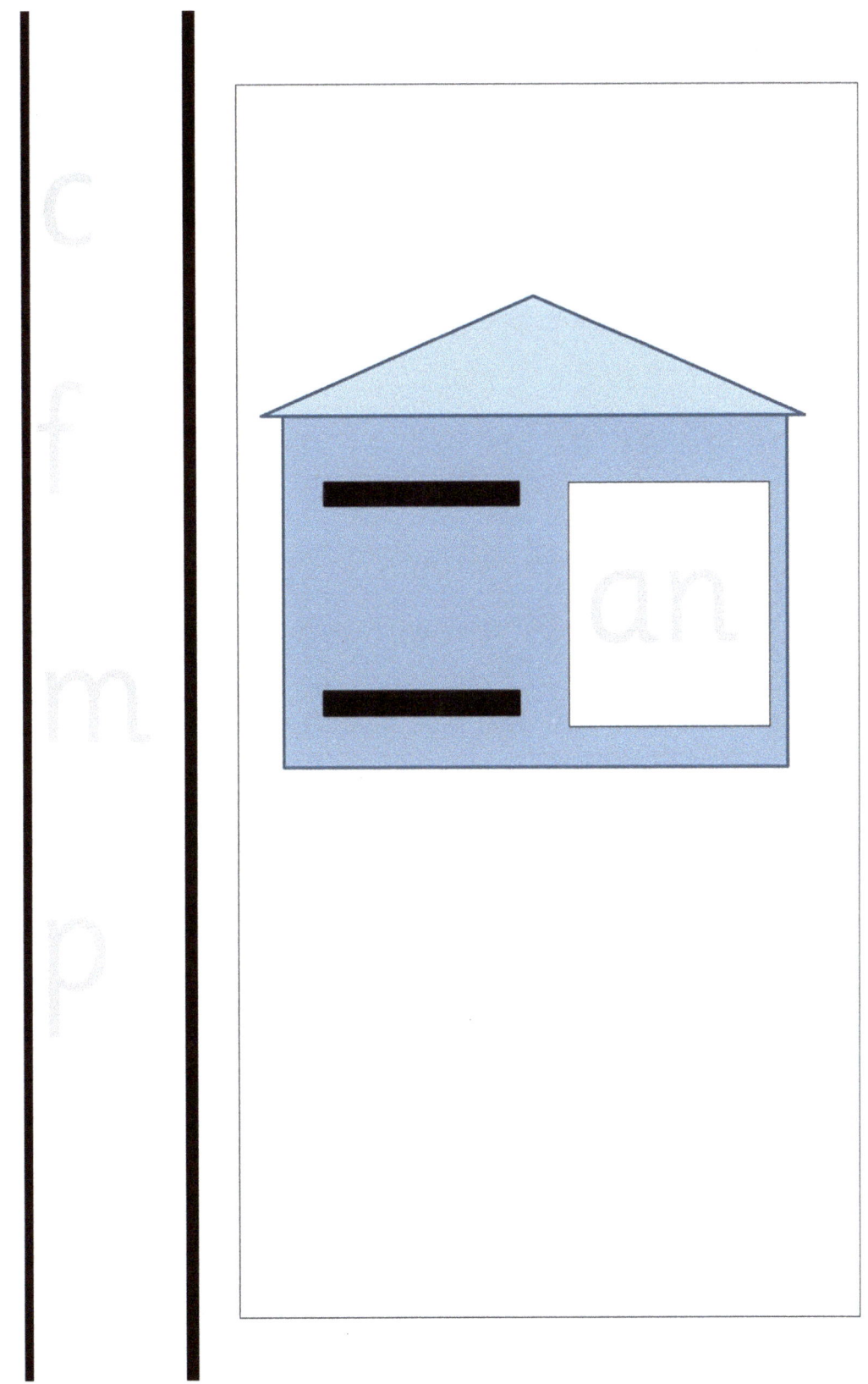

Cut along bold lines and feed through the window.

Pip 2

New word list:

pink	petal	her	there
sink	play	she	the
flower	put	it	you
under	will	on	see
Pip	with	by	help

Targeted phonics:

_nk
_in
fl_
_ll
_er

High frequency words:

her
she
it
on
by
the
there
you
will
with

Text:

1. the pond
2. there is a pink flower by the pond
3. look under the flower
4. can you see a weebee?
5. This is Pip   she is happy
6. Pip is pink and her petal is pink
7. Pip will play with her petal
8. she will put it on the pond
9. look the petal will sink
10. Grog can help

Book 2 Fish Pond (4 copies can be joined to make a rectangular 'pond')

Book 2 Fishing Lotto card 1

Book 2 fish for card 1

Attach either brass butterfly clips or simply use a staple for fishing with a magnet.

Book 2 Fishing Lotto card 2

Book 2 fish for card 2

Attach either brass butterfly clips or simply use a staple for fishing with a magnet.

Pip	play	will
Pip	play	will
put	petal	flower
put	petal	flower
she	pink	under
she	pink	under

Book 2 Memory game sheet 1

her	with	help
her	with	help
you	sink	there
you	sink	there
the	see	by
the	see	by

Book 2 Memory game sheet 2

Cut along bold lines and feed through the window

Tod 3

New word list:

hoots	jumps	they	peep
roots	deep	here	now
down	dark	Tod	skip
brown	up	an	have
owl	from	hop	fun

Targeted phonics:

br_
fr_
sk_
_ow
_ed

High frequency words:

they
here
now
down
up
an
have
from

Text:
1. the tree
2. look down there under the roots
3. deep down in the dark
4. here is a weebee   this is Tod
5. Tod is brown and his nest is brown
6. up in the tree an owl hoots
7. Tod jumps
8. he jumps down from his nest
9. Grog will play with Tod   they will jump and hop
10. Pip will play   she will peep at the owl
11. now Pip will jump and hop and skip
12. they will have fun

Tod		down
	deep	they
owl	roots	
hop		have
	fun	jumps
brown	now	

Book 3 Bingo sheet 1

owl		skip
	here	dark
Tod	roots	
down		peep
	brown	hoots
hop	have	

Book 3 Bingo sheet 2

hop		here
	skip	fun
brown	roots	
now		deep
	they	jumps
Tod	owl	

down		skip
	from	fun
deep	brown	
now		Tod
	have	jumps
here	they	

Book 3 Bingo sheet 4

Tod	down	deep
owl	have	dark
now	roots	hoots
fun	here	skip
brown	they	jumps
hop	peep	from

Book 3 Bingo word sheet

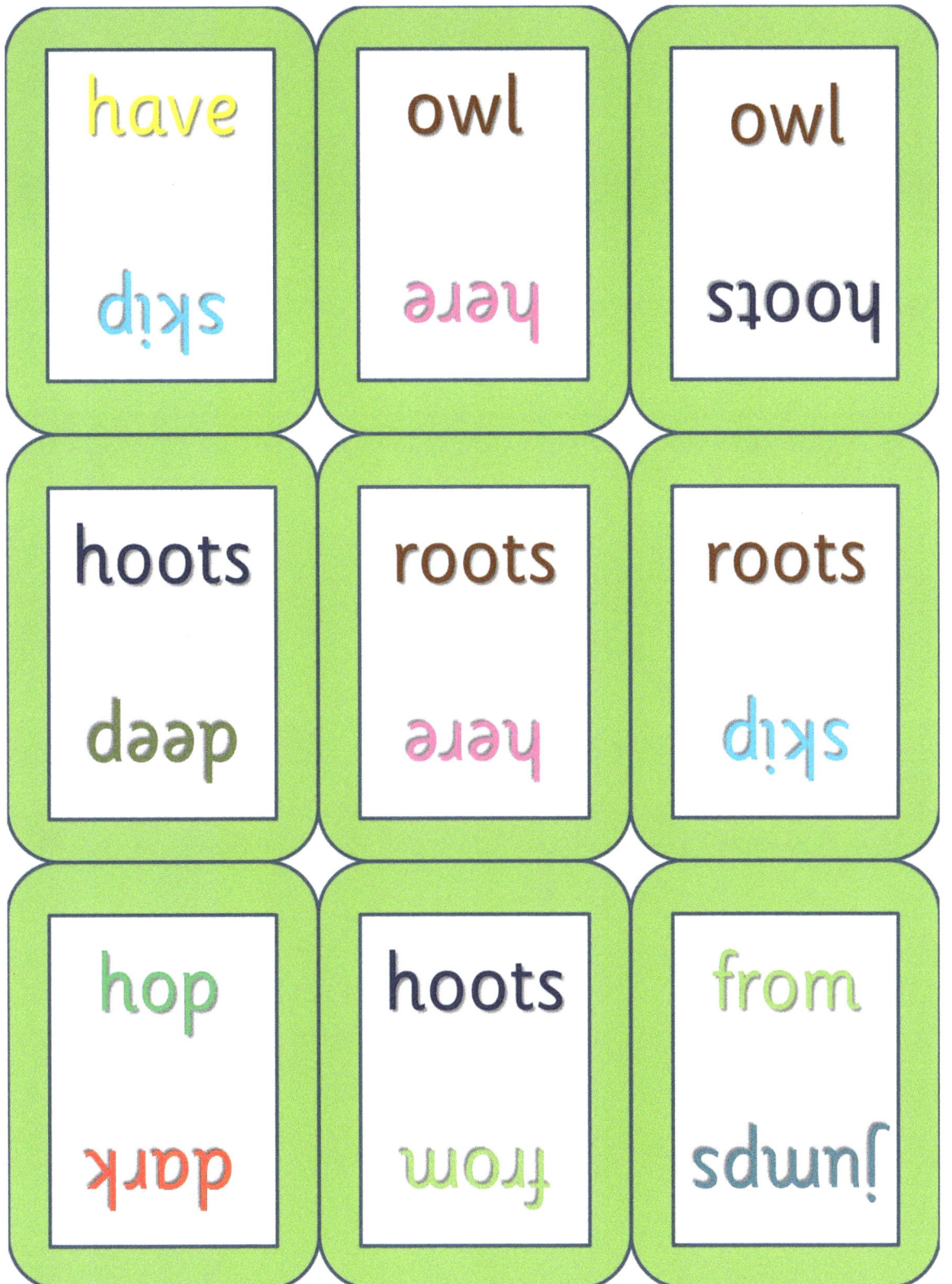

Book 3 Dominoes sheet 1

weebee Series 1 (Books 1-8) Complete Resource Book

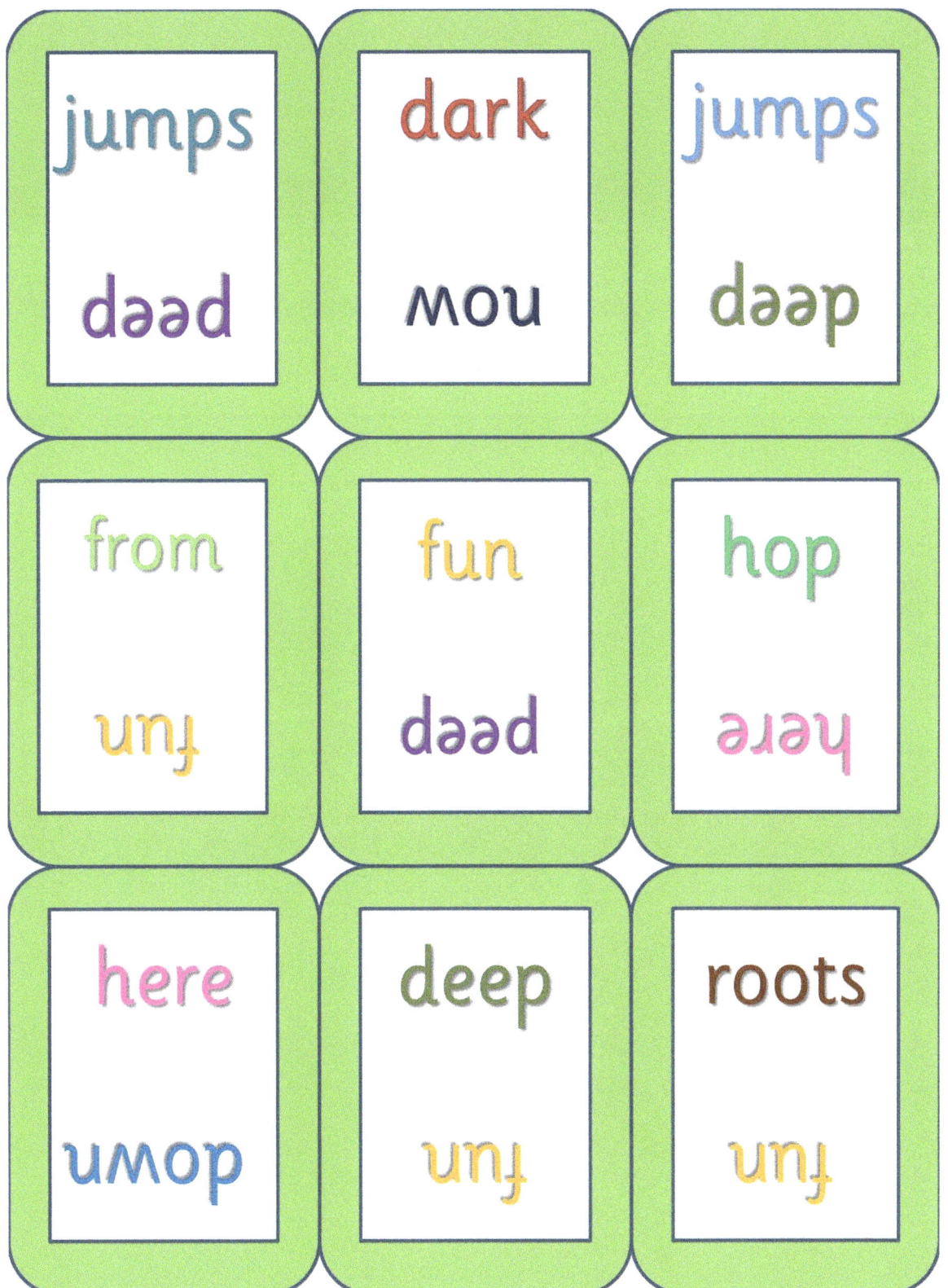

Book 3 Dominoes sheet 2

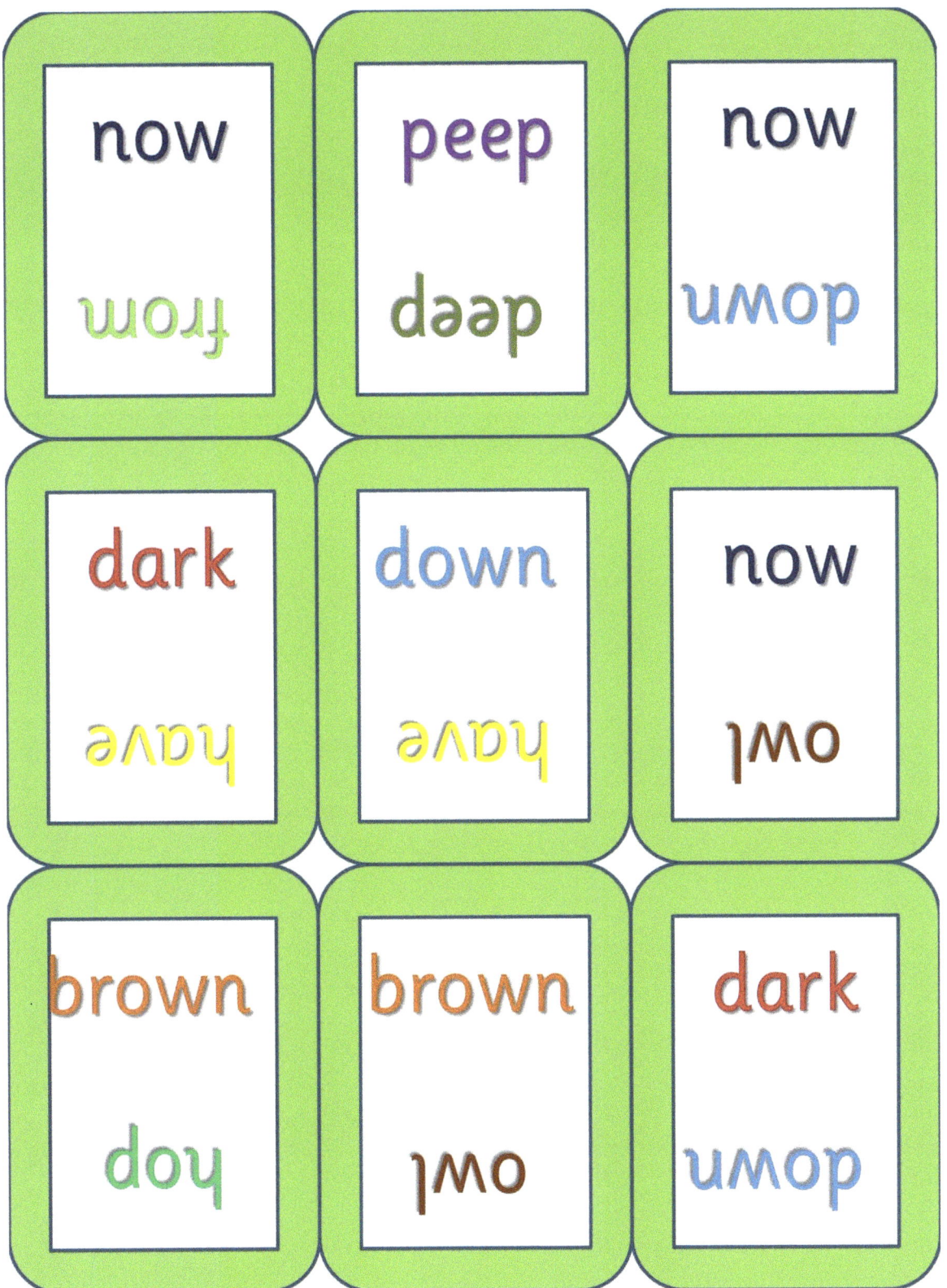

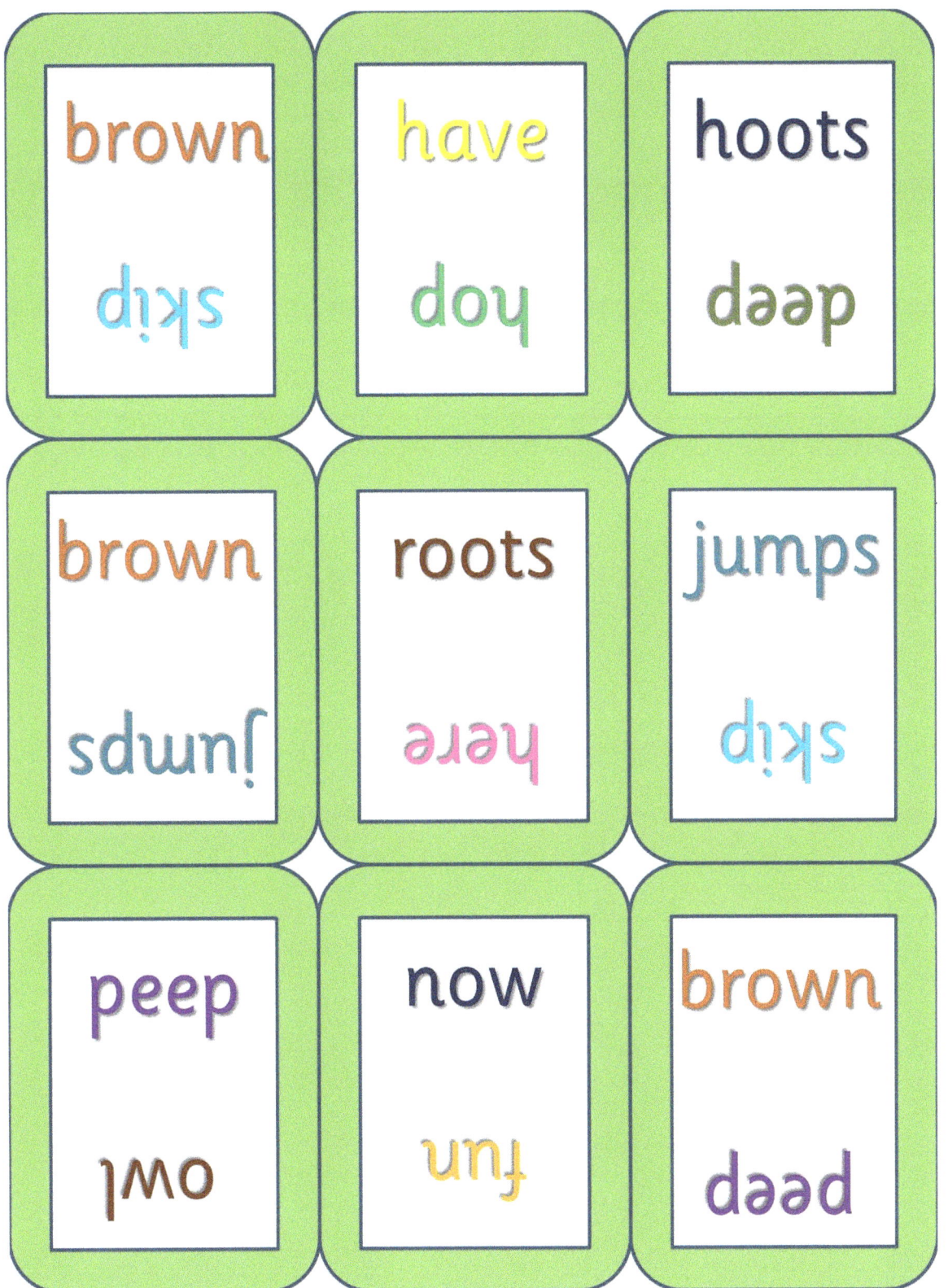

Book 3 Dominoes sheet 4

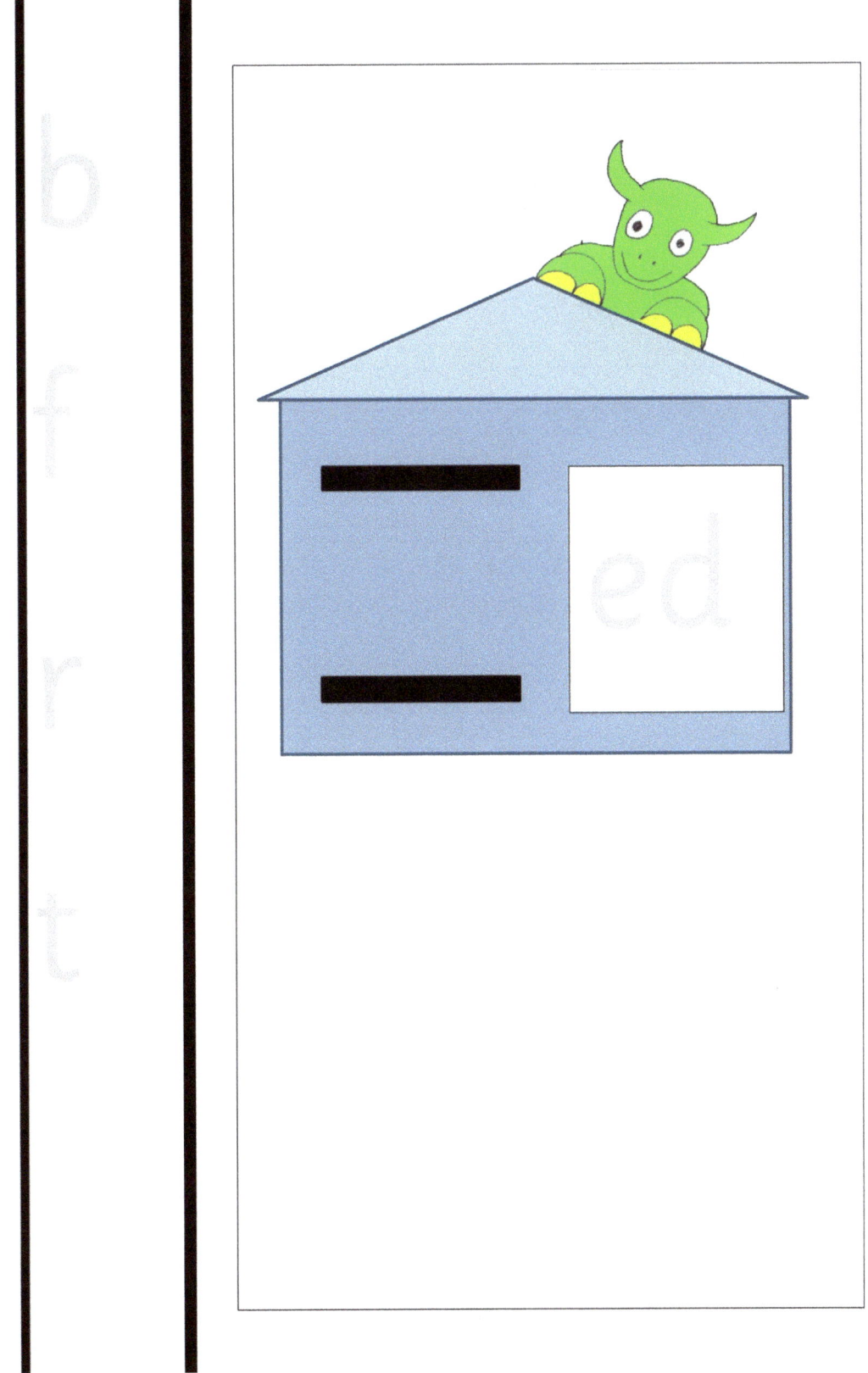

Cut along bold lines and feed through the window

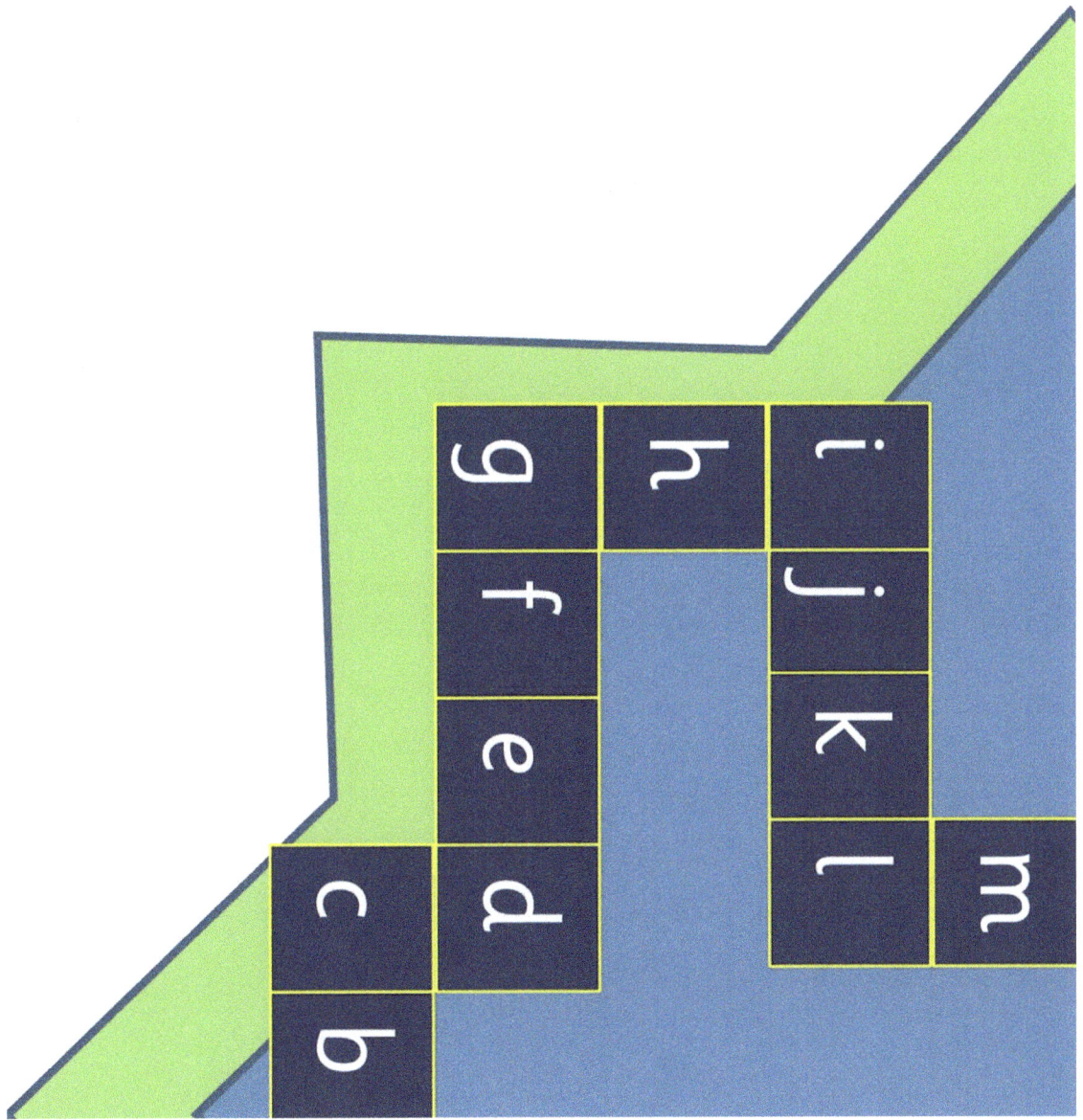

Lower left section of Octologo Board
This needs to be joined to the other three sections. The board can be re-used for each book.

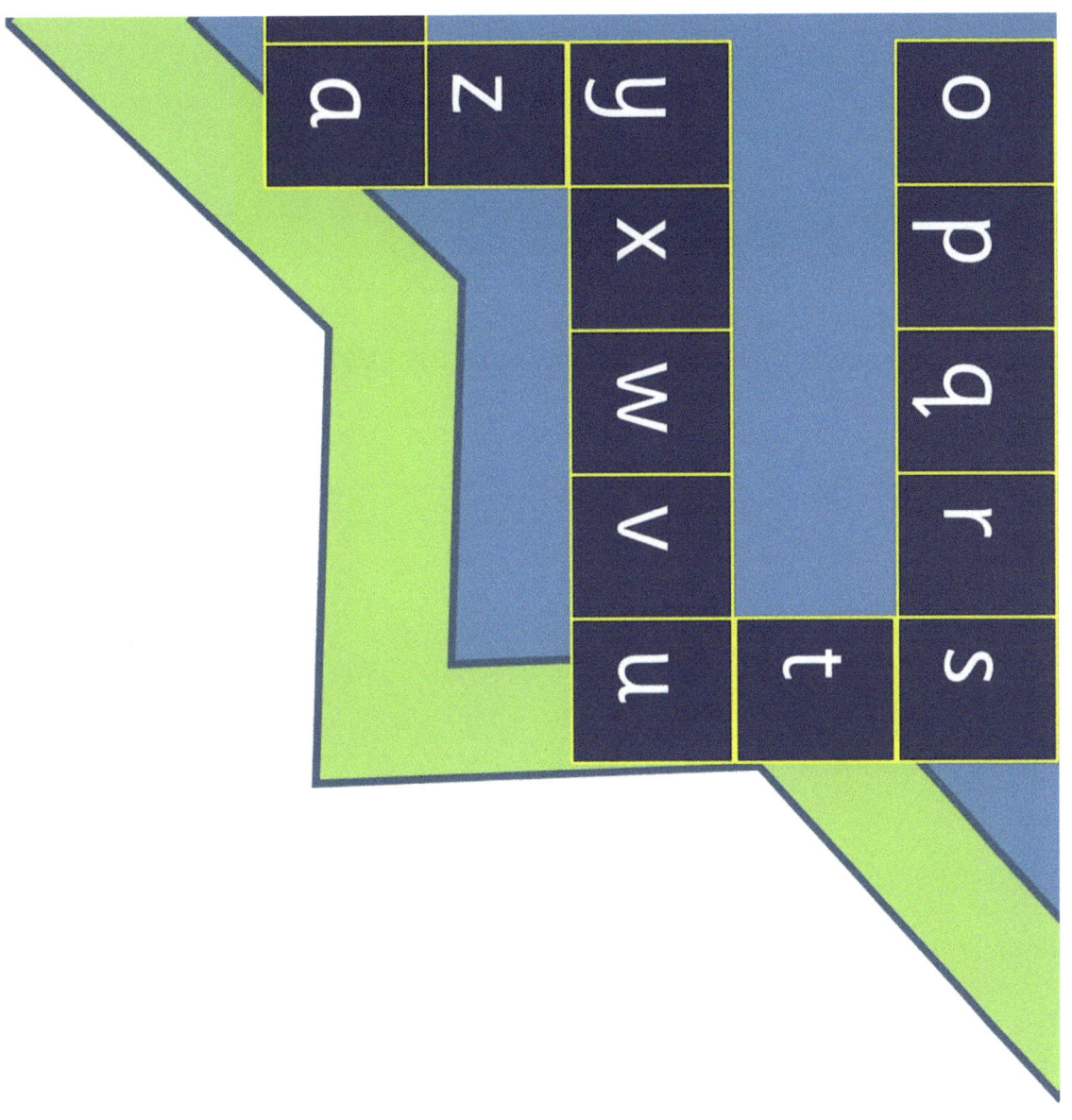

Lower right section of Octologo Board
This needs to be joined to the other three sections. The board can be re-used for each book.

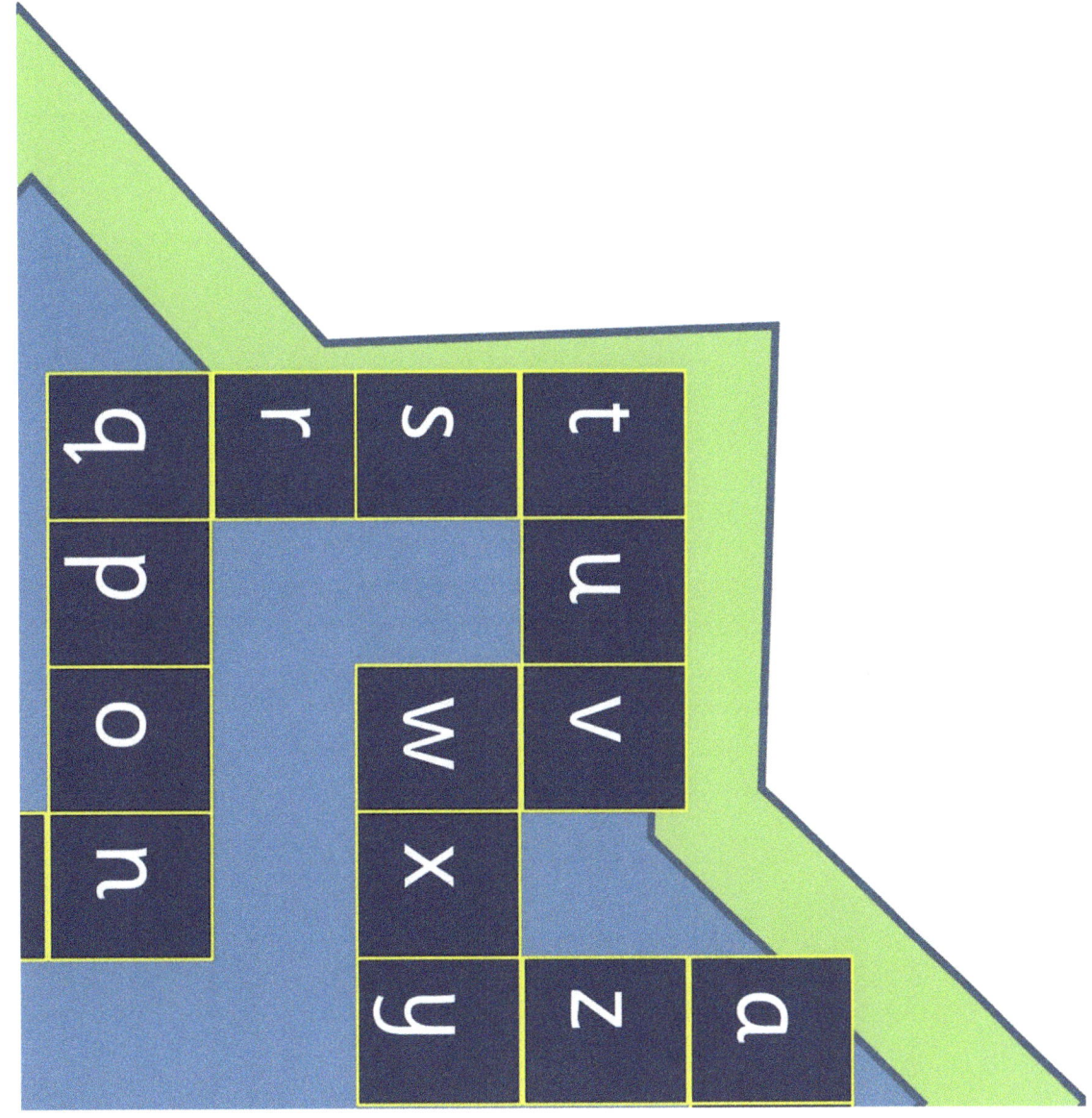

Upper left section of Octologo Board
This needs to be joined to the other three sections. The board can be re-used for each book.

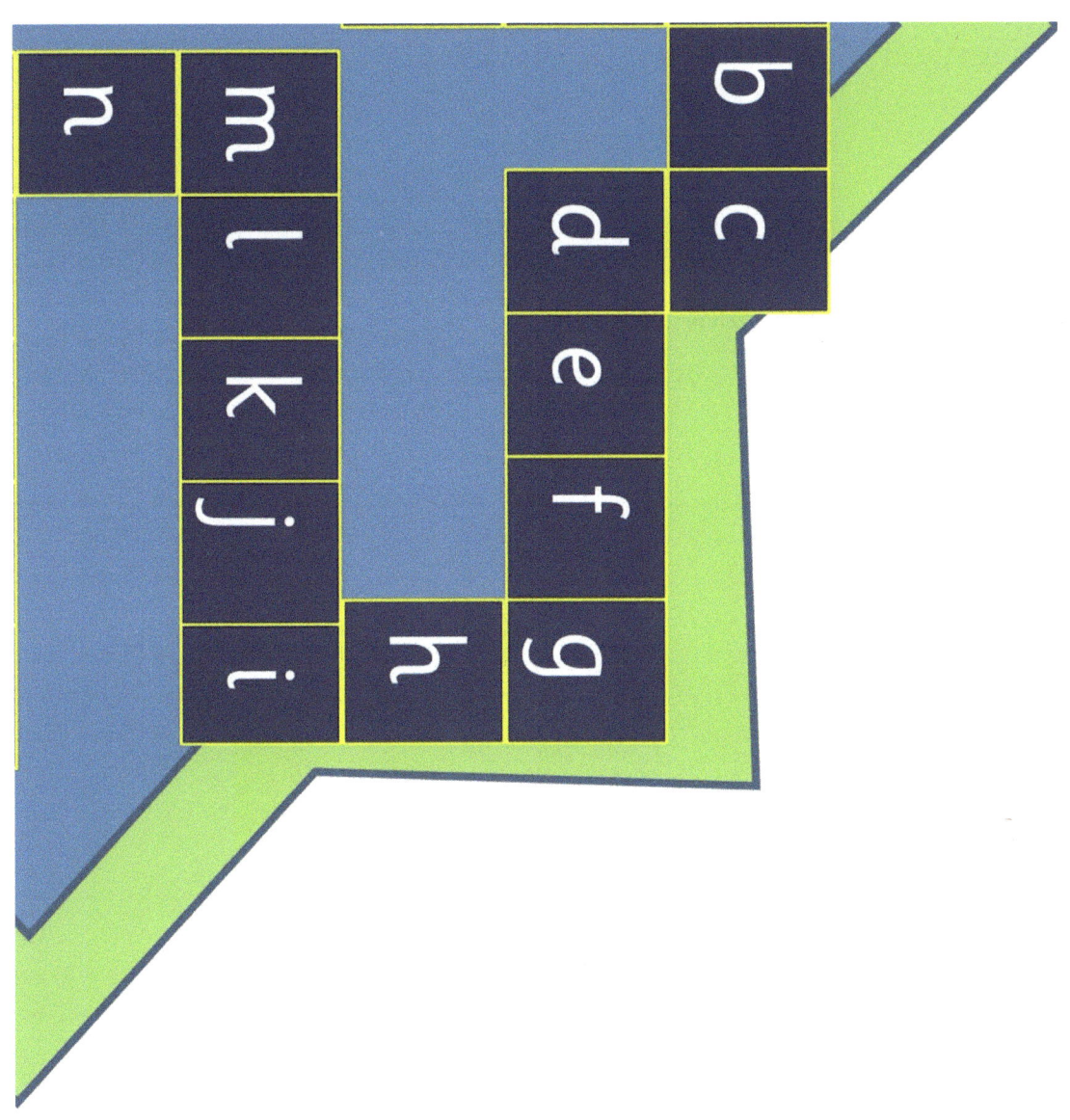

Upper right section of Octologo Board
This needs to be joined to the other three sections. The board can be re-used for each book.

Octologo player's board
You will need one board per player. Using dice, take turns to move around the board alphabetically. If there is a word on the table that begins with the same letter that has been landed on, the player may take it and put it on their board. The winner is the first to fill their board.

owl	brown	down	roots	hoots
from	up	dark	deep	jumps
hop	an	Tod	here	they
fun	have	skip	now	peep

Book 3 Octologo word sheet
Print 1 for each player

Mop 4

New Word list:

long	grip	onto	sing
song	Mop	has	swing
been	big	as	but
for	grass	well	too
swim	yellow	bow	low

Targeted phonics:

_ng
_ll
_ss
_ow
sw_

High frequency words:

been
for
big
has
as
well
but

Text:
1. the big brown tree
2. look down there by the long grass
3. can you see a yellow flower?
4. there is a weebee under the yellow flower
5. this weebee is Mop   she is yellow and green   she can sing a song
6. Mop can grip onto the flower and sing
7. Grog has been for a swim   he will play with Mop under the yellow flower
8. Pip will play as well   she has a bow
9. the bow is fun   Mop can skip
10. Tod will play as well   he will swing on the bow
11. but the bow is too low

Book 4 Fishing Lotto card 1

Book 4 fish for card 1

Attach either brass butterfly clips or simply use a staple for fishing with a magnet.

Book 4 fish for card 2

Attach either brass butterfly clips or simply use a staple for fishing with a magnet.

Mop	long	song
Mop	long	song
big	grass	swim
big	grass	swim
grip	onto	swing
grip	onto	swing

Book 4 Memory game sheet 1

low	been	sing
low	been	sing
for	yellow	well
for	yellow	well
bow	but	too
bow	but	too

Book 4 Memory game sheet 2

Book 4 Happy Word Families sheet 1

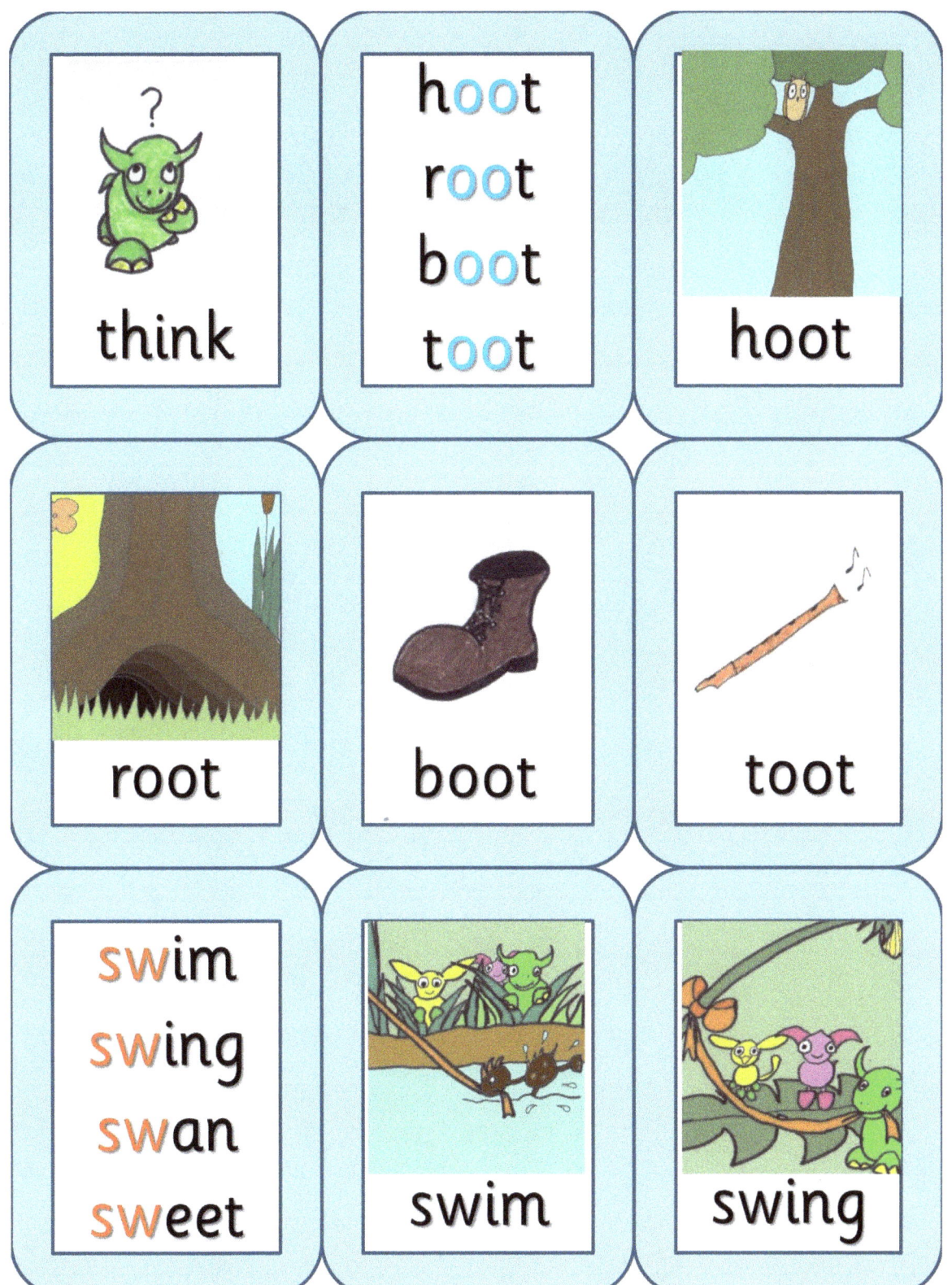

Book 4 Happy Word Families sheet 2

Happy Word Families (for 4 players)

- Give each player a master card (with a list of words)

- These cards are placed face up in front of the player

- The remaining cards are shuffled and shared out equally

- Players take turns clockwise to ask another player if they have a card from their family

- If they have the requested card they must hand it over

- If they do not have the requested card, it is the next player's turn

- The winner is the first to collect the whole of their family

Book 4 Happy Word Families sheet 3

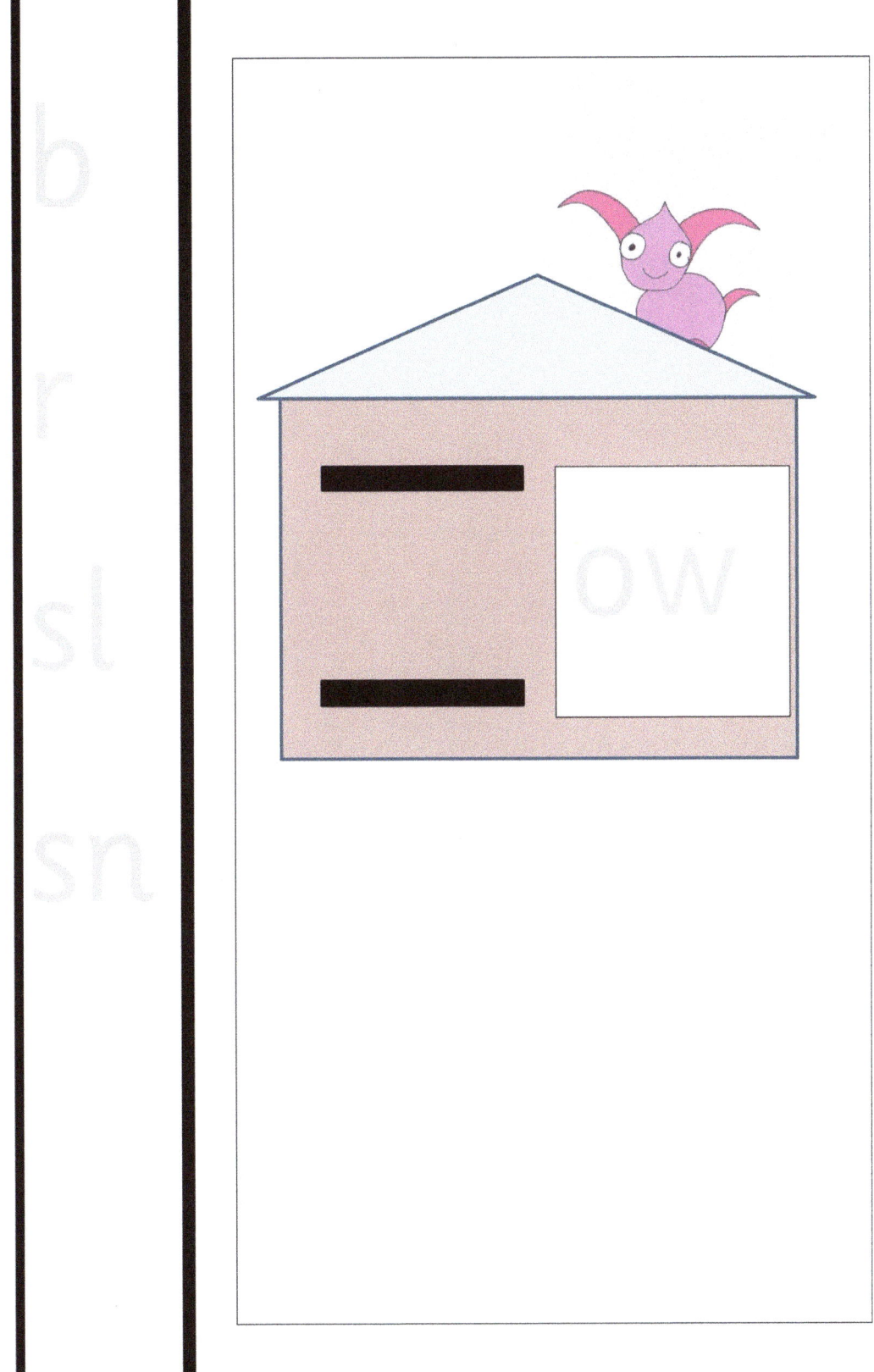

Cut along bold lines and feed through the window

long	grip	onto	sing
song	mop	has	swing
been	big	as	but
for	grass	well	too
swim	yellow	bow	low

Book 4 Octologo word sheet
Print 1 for each player

Jig 5

Words list:

top	to	had	wings
of	no	luck	stick
Jig	not	old	slip
blue	rock	sack	land
go	duck	bug	soft

Targeted phonics:

_ck
_ld
_ip
sl_
bl_

High frequency words:

to
had
of
no
go
not
old

Text:
1. up at the top of the tree is a weebee
2. this weebee is Jig; she is as big as a bug
3. Jig is blue and yellow; she has wings
4. Grog and Mop will go to look for Jig
5. Pip and Tod will go to look for Jig as well
6. no, Grog will not see Jig on the rock
7. no, Pip will not see Jig with the duck
8. and Tod has no luck
9. now Jig is on the old sack
10. Mop can see Jig on top of the old blue sack
11. Grog will go up the stick to the top of the sack
12. the weebees go up the stick
13. it is fun to slip down the sack
14. they land in the soft grass

weebee Series 1 (Books 1-8) Complete Resource Book

Jig		luck
	slip	blue
top	wings	
bug		stick
	not	duck
no	old	

Book 5 Bingo sheet 1

slip		had
	duck	soft
go	land	
Jig		luck
	not	blue
top	bug	

Book 5 Bingo sheet 2

Jig		old
	slip	had
no	sack	
top		land
	bug	stick
duck	luck	

Book 5 Bingo sheet 3

not		luck
	blue	old
Jig	rock	
go		slip
	had	stick
bug	duck	

Book 5 Bingo sheet 4

Jig	luck	slip
top	blue	duck
bug	stick	soft
no	land	had
not	rock	wings
go	sack	old

Book 5 Bingo word sheet

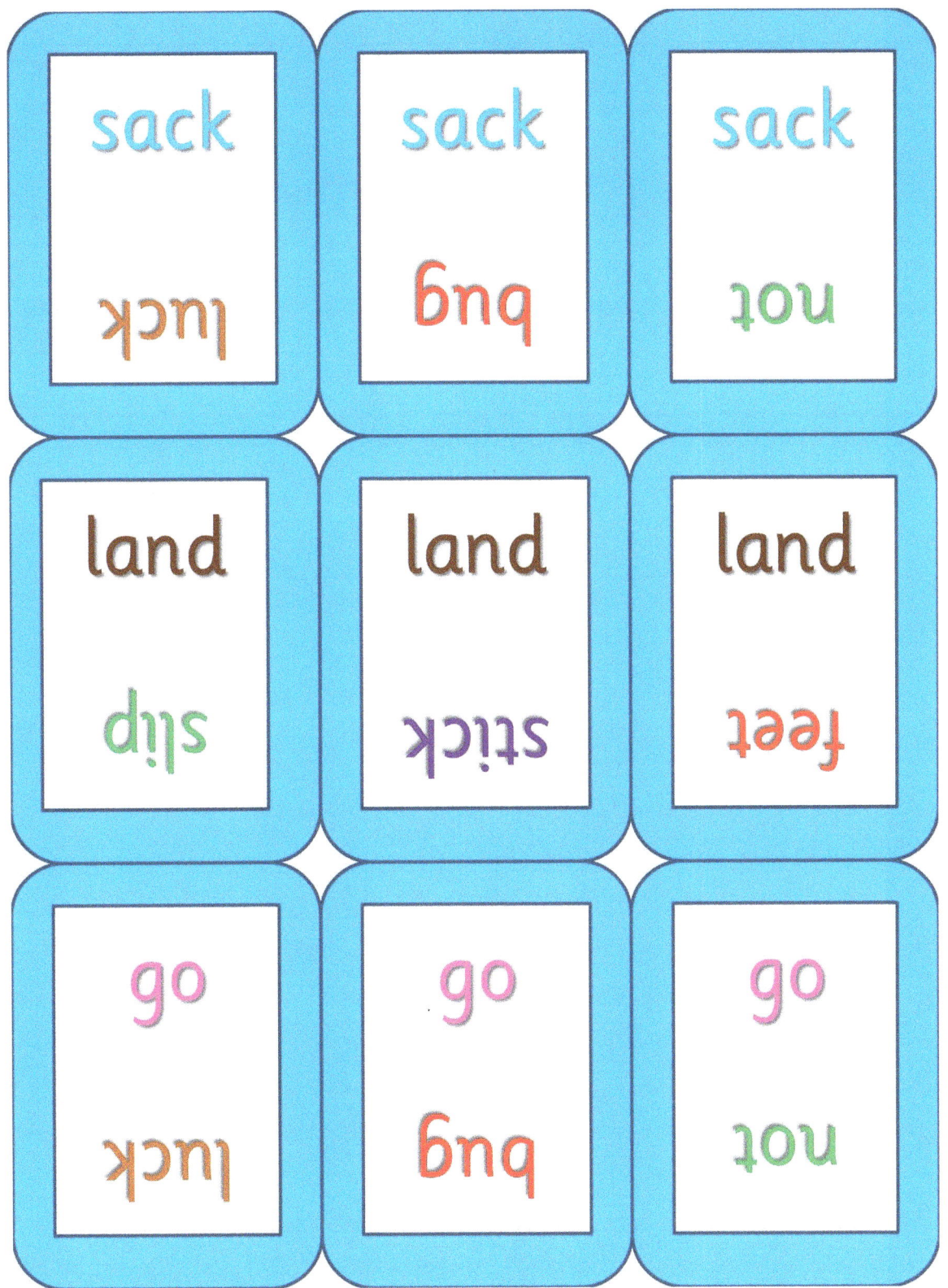

Book 5 Dominoes sheet 1

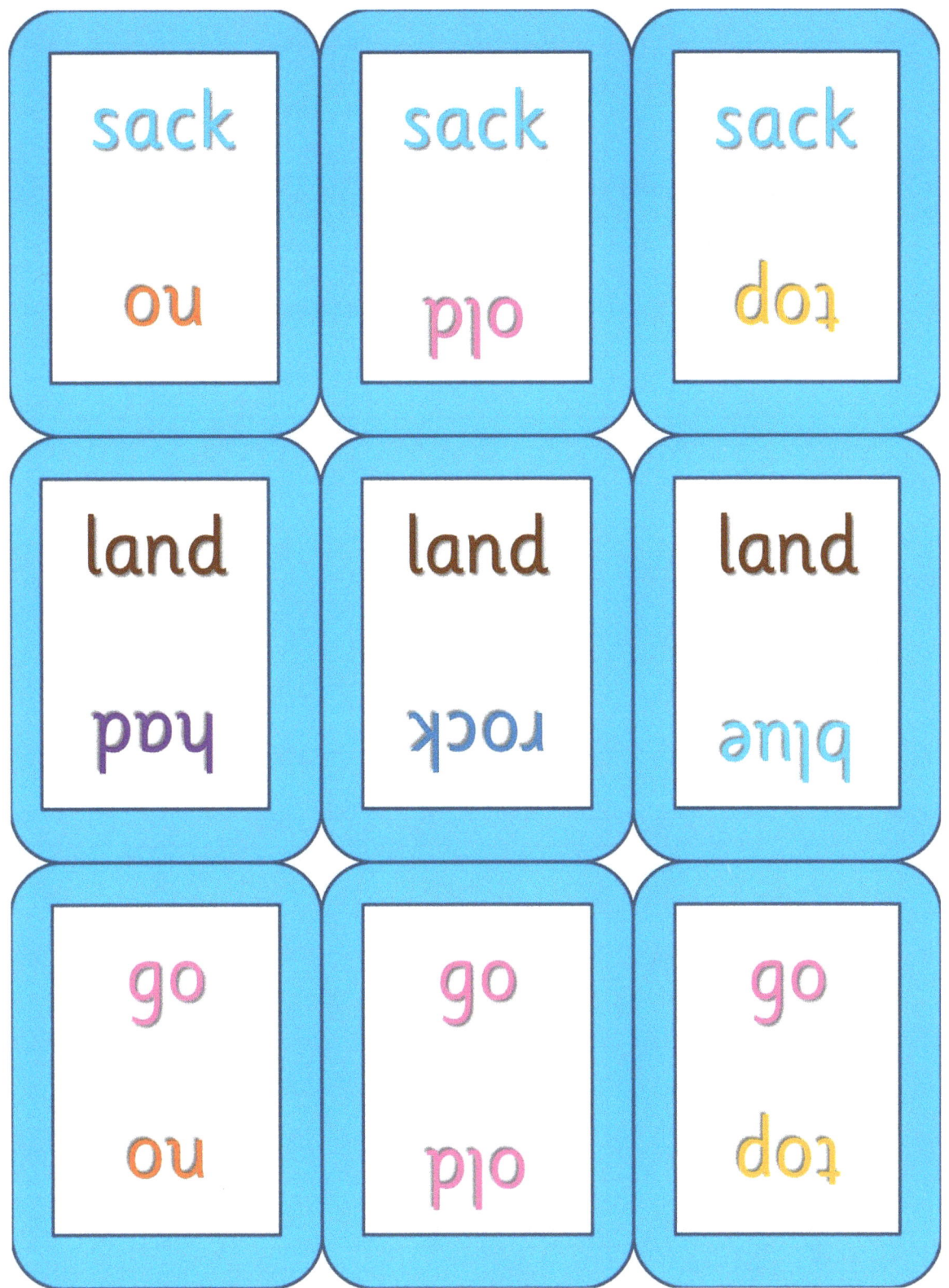

Book 5 Dominoes sheet 2

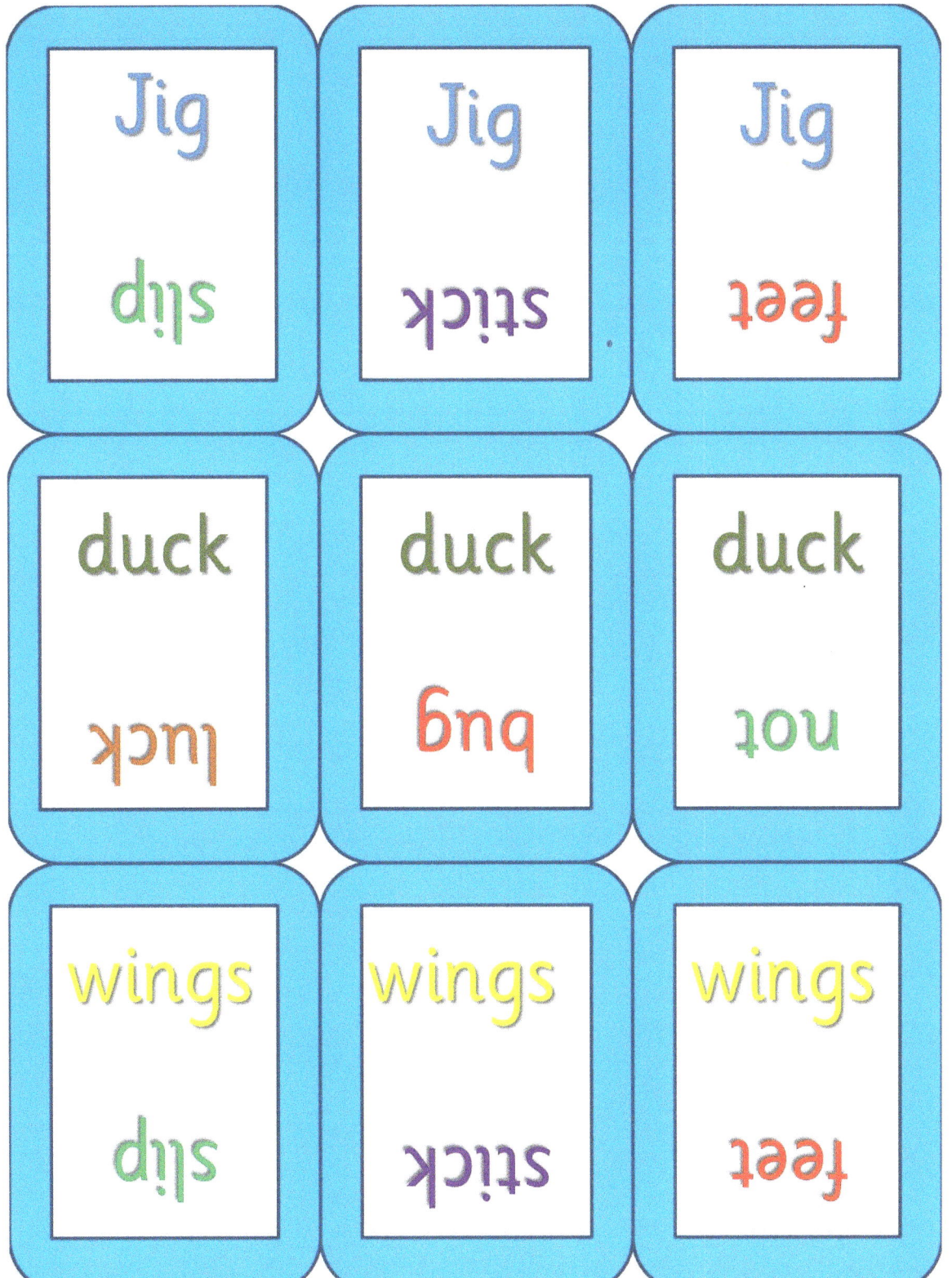

Book 5 Dominoes sheet 3

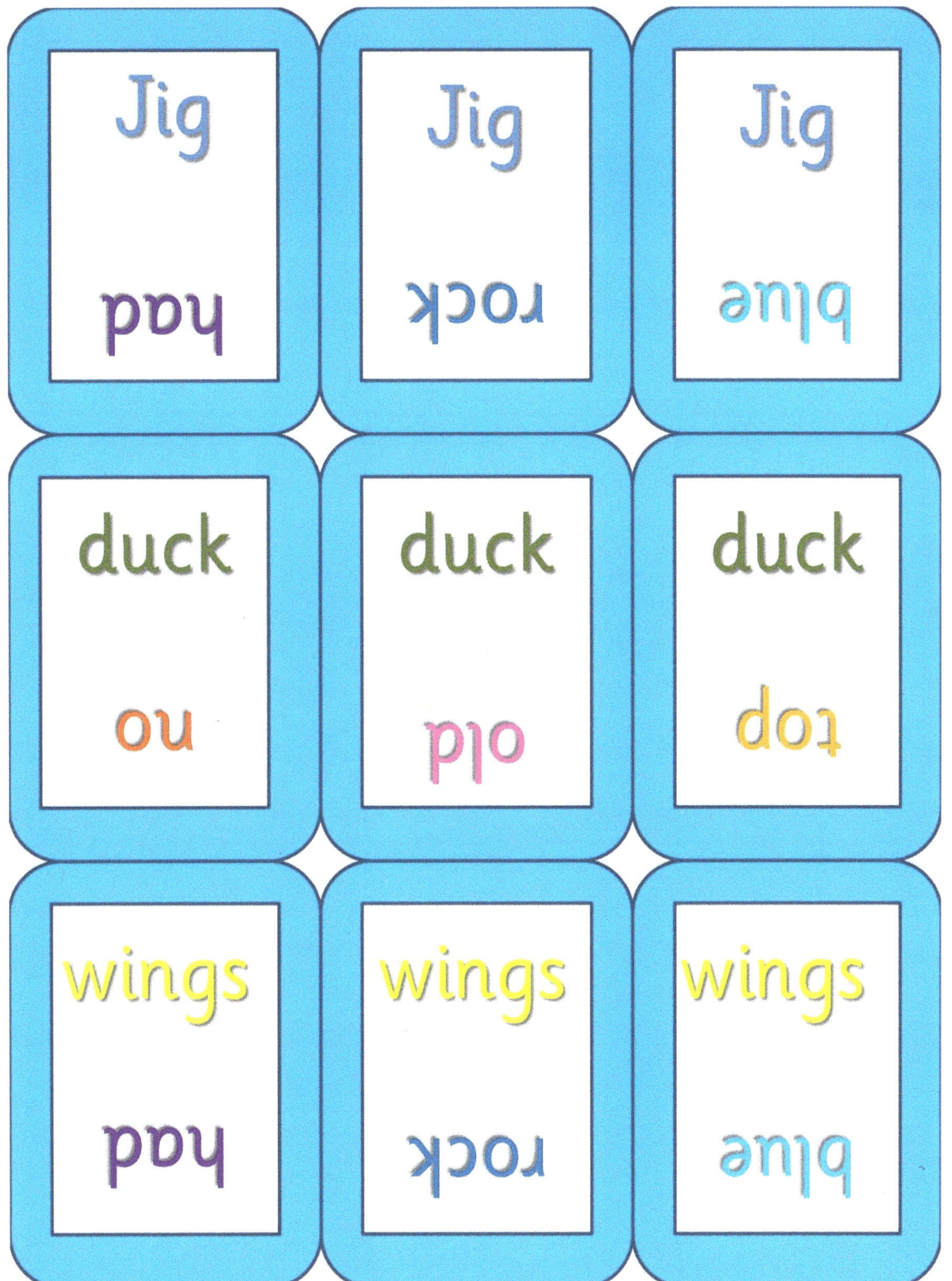

Book 5 Dominoes sheet 4

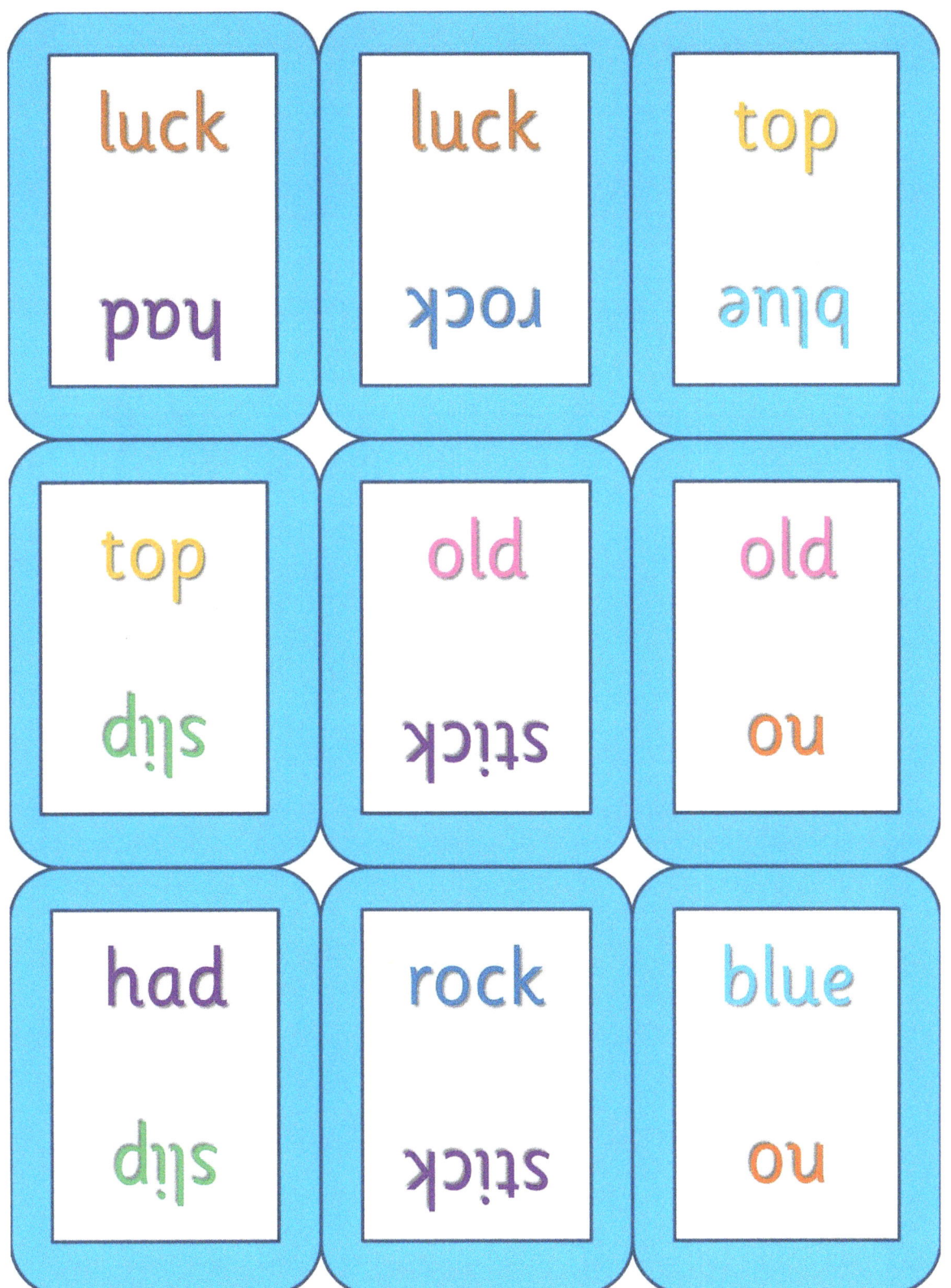

Book 5 Dominoes sheet 5

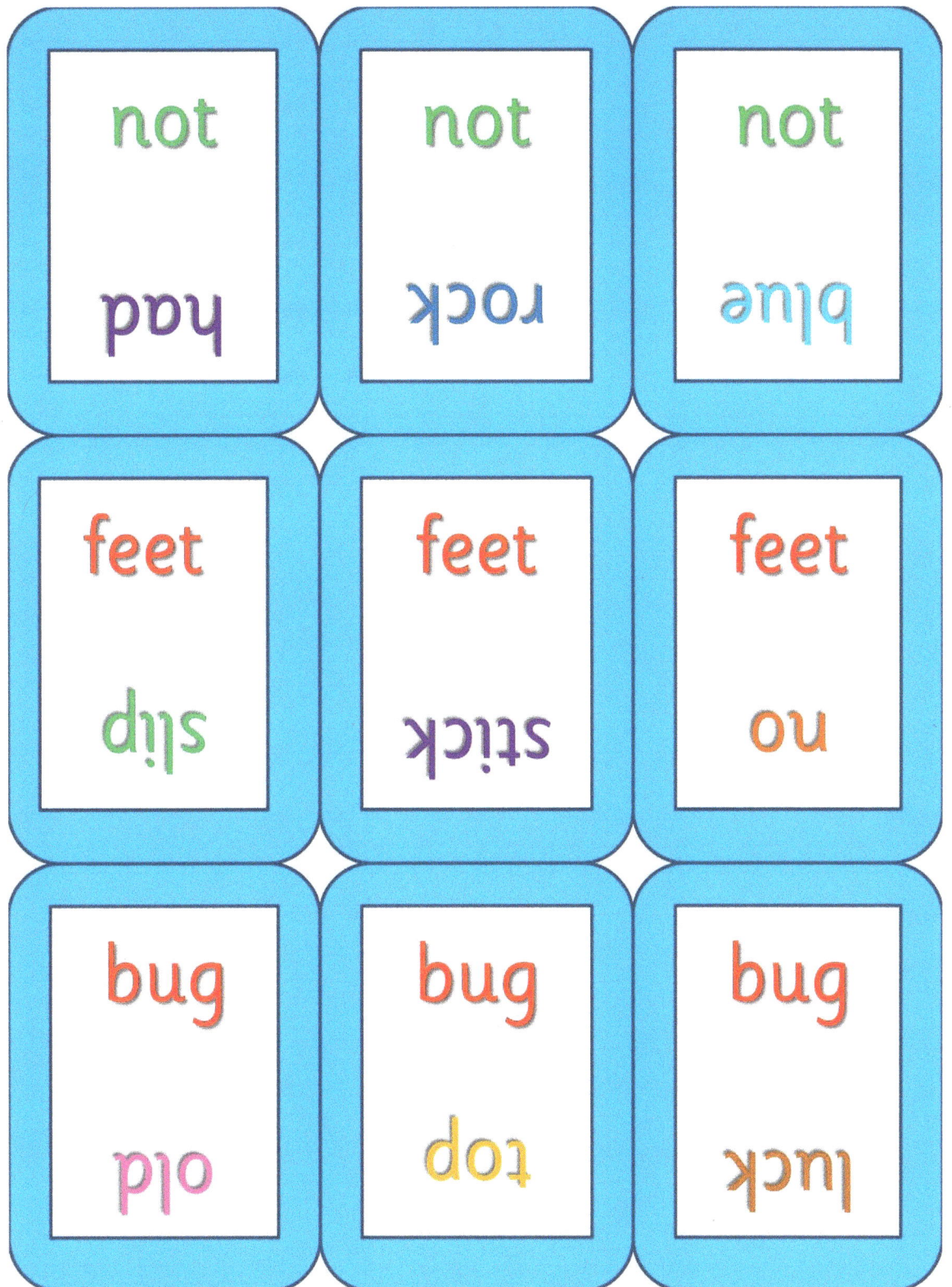

Book 5 Dominoes sheet 6

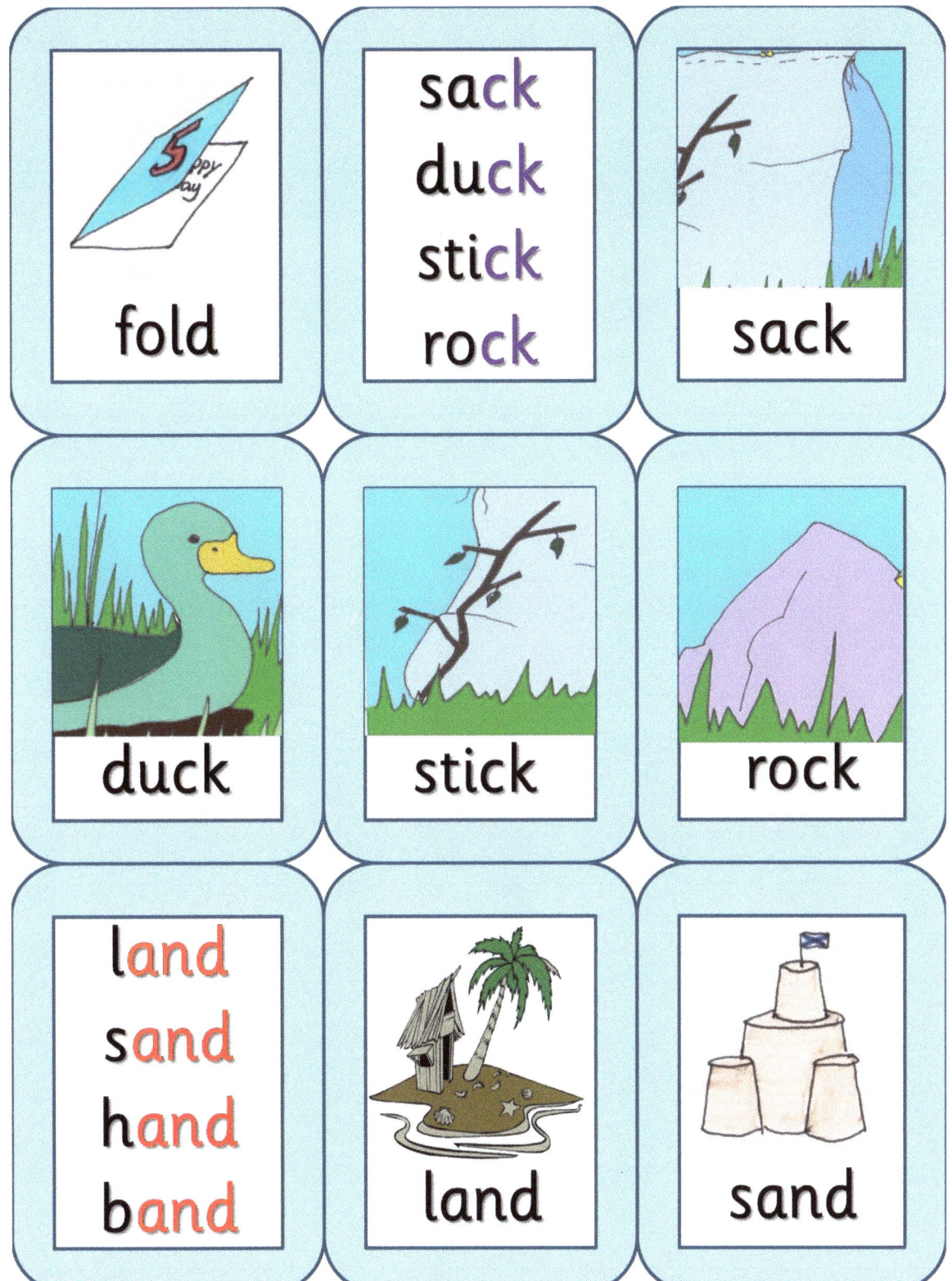

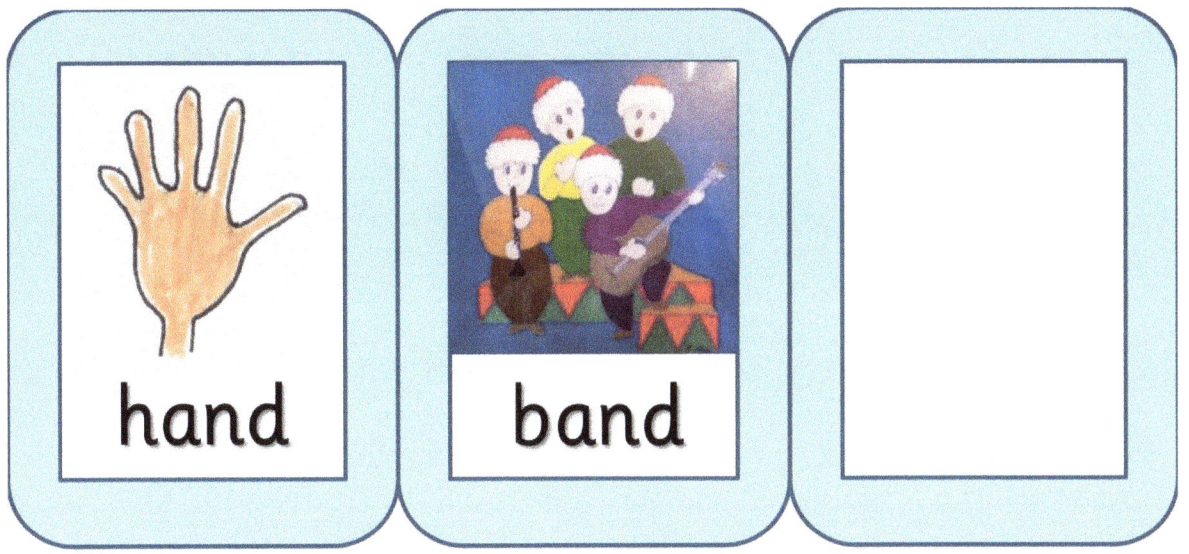

Happy Word Families (for 4 players)

- Give each player a master card (with a list of words)

- These cards are placed face up in front of the player

- The remaining cards are shuffled and shared out equally

- Players take turns clockwise to ask another player if they have a card from their family

- If they have the requested card they must hand it over

- If they do not have the requested card, it is the next player's turn

- The winner is the first to collect the whole of their family

Book 5 Happy Word Families sheet 3

Cut along bold lines and feed through the window

top	of	Jig	blue	go
to	no	not	rock	duck
had	luck	old	sack	bug
wings	stick	slip	land	soft

Book 5 Octologo word sheet
Print 1 for each player

Zon 6

Word list:

fall	star	sky	flash
tall	moon	fly	crash
wall	Zon	cry	ship
small	get	try	shell
miss	back	metal	upset

Targeted phonics:

_ar
_all
_sh_
_y
_it

High frequency words:

get
back

Text:
1. a yellow star
2. the yellow moon
3. the blue sky
4. this weebee is Zon; his ship can fly
5. crash! Zon will fall
6. the ship will land by the tall tree
7. the grass is soft; Zon is not upset
8. flash! Zon is upset but he will not cry
9. Grog is by an old wall; he can see Zon; he will go to help
10. Zon is small but Jig can see him from up in the tree
11. the metal ship will not fly; Zon will not get back to his star
12. Grog will help Zon look for a nest
13. Jig can see an old shell
14. Zon can sleep in the shell; he will not miss his ship; he is happy

Book 6 Fishing Lotto card 1

Book 6 Fishing Lotto card 2

Book 6 fish for card 1

Attach either brass butterfly clips or simply use a staple for fishing with a magnet.

Book 6 fish for card 2

Attach either brass butterfly clips or simply use a staple for fishing with a magnet.

back	fly	sky
back	fly	sky
cry	metal	flash
cry	metal	flash
try	crash	ship
try	crash	ship

Book 6 Memory game sheet 2

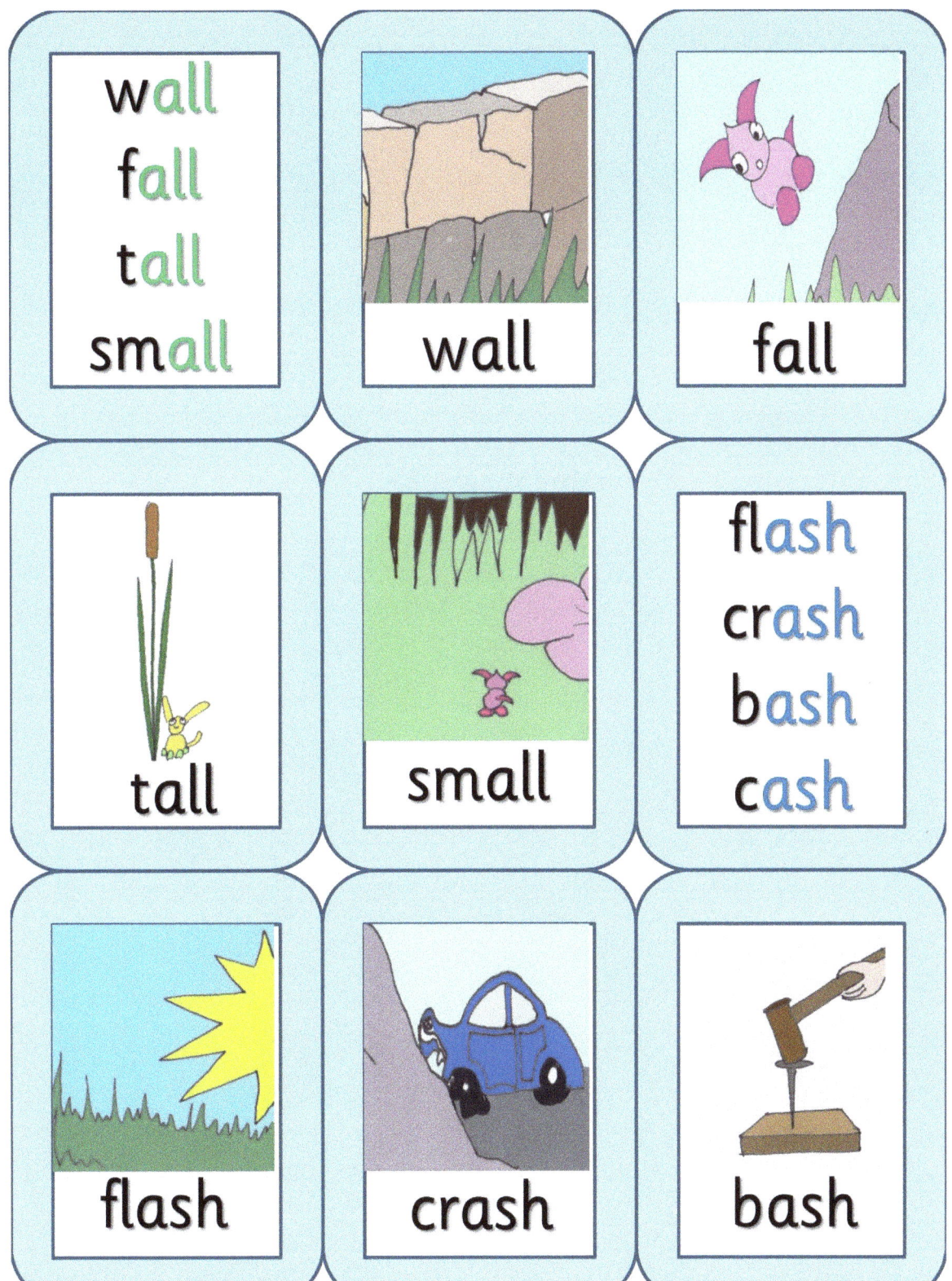

Happy Word Families (for 4 players)

- Give each player a master card (with a list of words)

- These cards are placed face up in front of the player

- The remaining cards are shuffled and shared out equally

- Players take turns clockwise to ask another player if they have a card from their family

- If they have the requested card they must hand it over

- If they do not have the requested card, it is the next player's turn

- The winner is the first to collect the whole of their family

Book 6 Happy Word Families sheet 3

Cut along bold lines and feed through the window

miss	small	wall	tall	fall
back	get	Zon	moon	star
metal	try	cry	fly	sky
upset	shell	ship	crash	flash

Book 6 Octologo word sheet
Print 1 for each player

Flup 7

Word list:

hat	going	button	Flup	so
run	tell	bed	sit	off
them	wood	man	box	bit
fix	very	grey	good	fluff

Targeted phonics:

fl-
_ff
_ood
_x
_og

High frequency words:

so
off
them

Text:
1. The old wall.
2. An old soft hat.
3. This weebee is Flup. He can sit in his nest. Flup is red and grey.
4. Zon can see a man in a hat. The man looks very big.
5. Zon is going to run off to look for Grog.
6. Grog is with Tod by an old metal box in the wood.
7. Pip is in the grey metal bow. She has a blue button.
8. Zon will tell Grog to see the man.
9. Grog, Tod and Pip will go with Zon. They will see the big man with the old hat.
10. Tod can see Flup in his nest. Flup will fly down to see them.
11. Now zon can see Flup and his nest.
12. Flup will get a bit of fluff for Zon. Zon will have a soft bed.
13. The blue button will look good on the man. Flup can fix it.
14. Flup is very happy.

hat		run
	them	fix
tell	going	
very		wood
	bed	button
man	grey	

Book 7 Bingo sheet 1

box		sit
	Flup	off
good	fluff	
hat		run
	them	going
fix	tell	

Book 7 Bingo sheet 2

hat		run
	fluff	them
off	going	
fix		very
	grey	wood
good	Flup	

tell		wood
	good	very
bed	grey	
man		Flup
	sit	off
fluff	button	

Book 7 Bingo sheet 4

hat	run	them
fix	going	tell
button	very	wood
sit	bed	man
grey	Flup	box
off	fluff	good

Book 7 Bingo word sheet

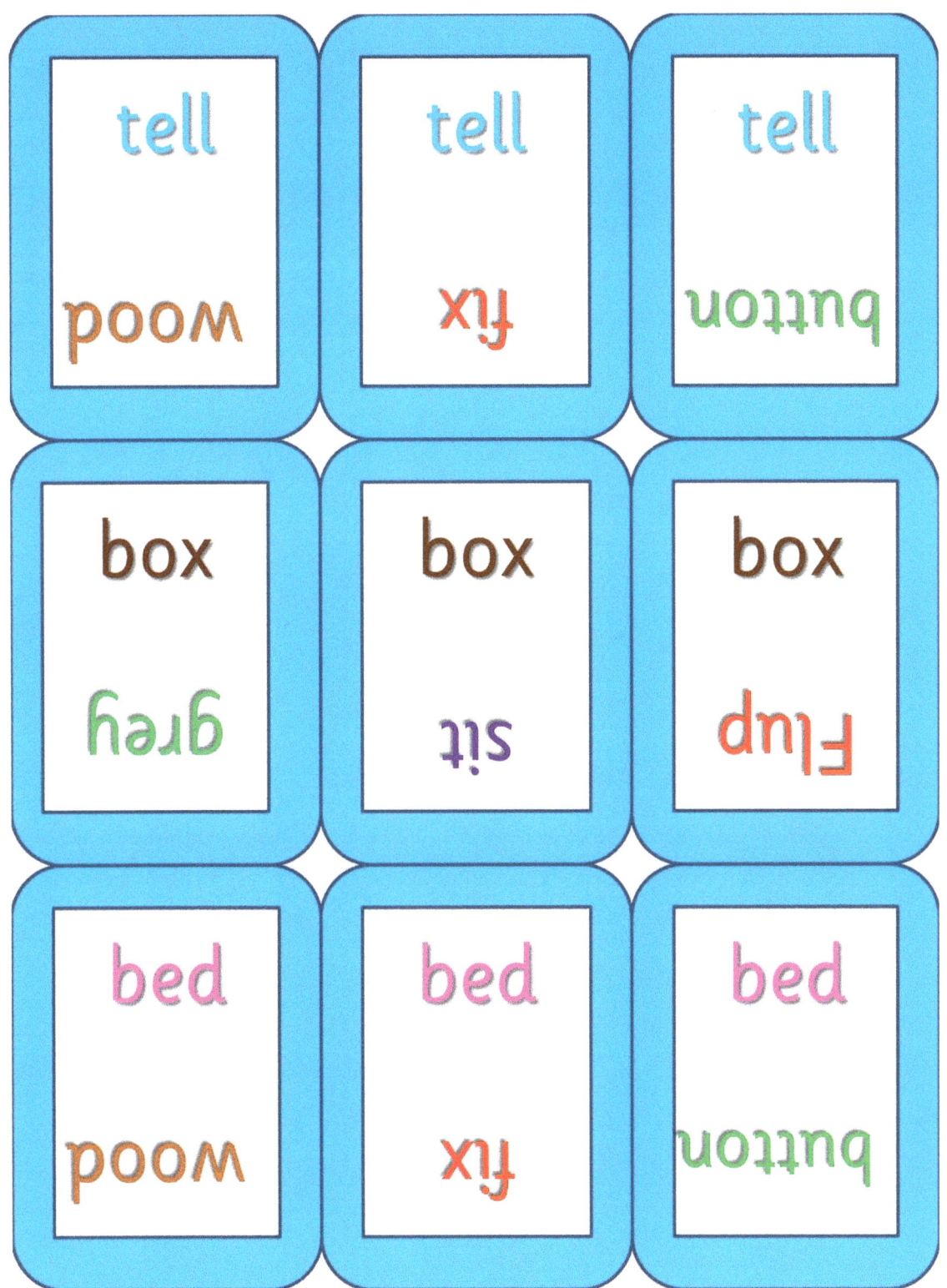

Book 7 Dominoes sheet 1

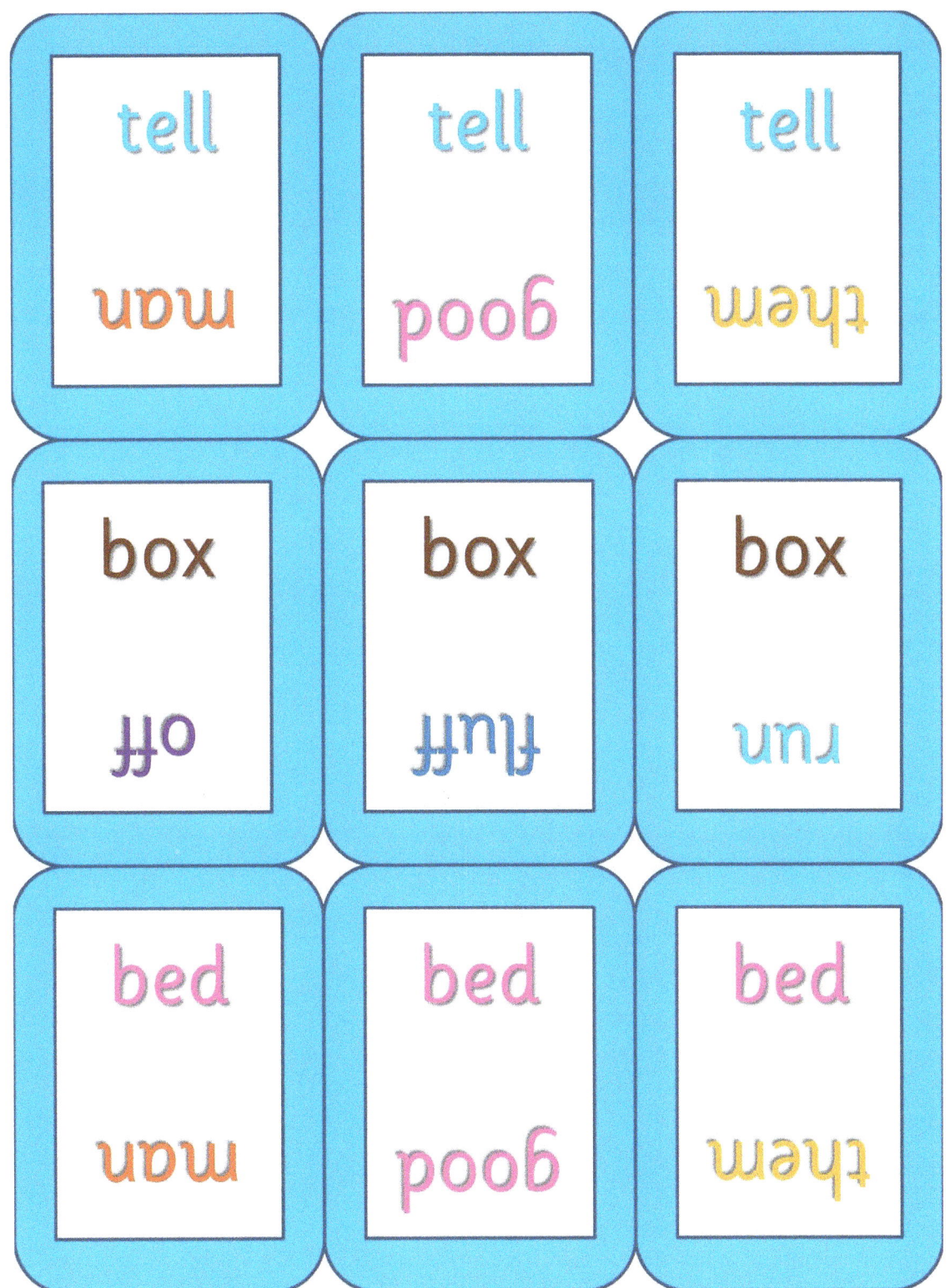

Book 7 Dominoes sheet 2

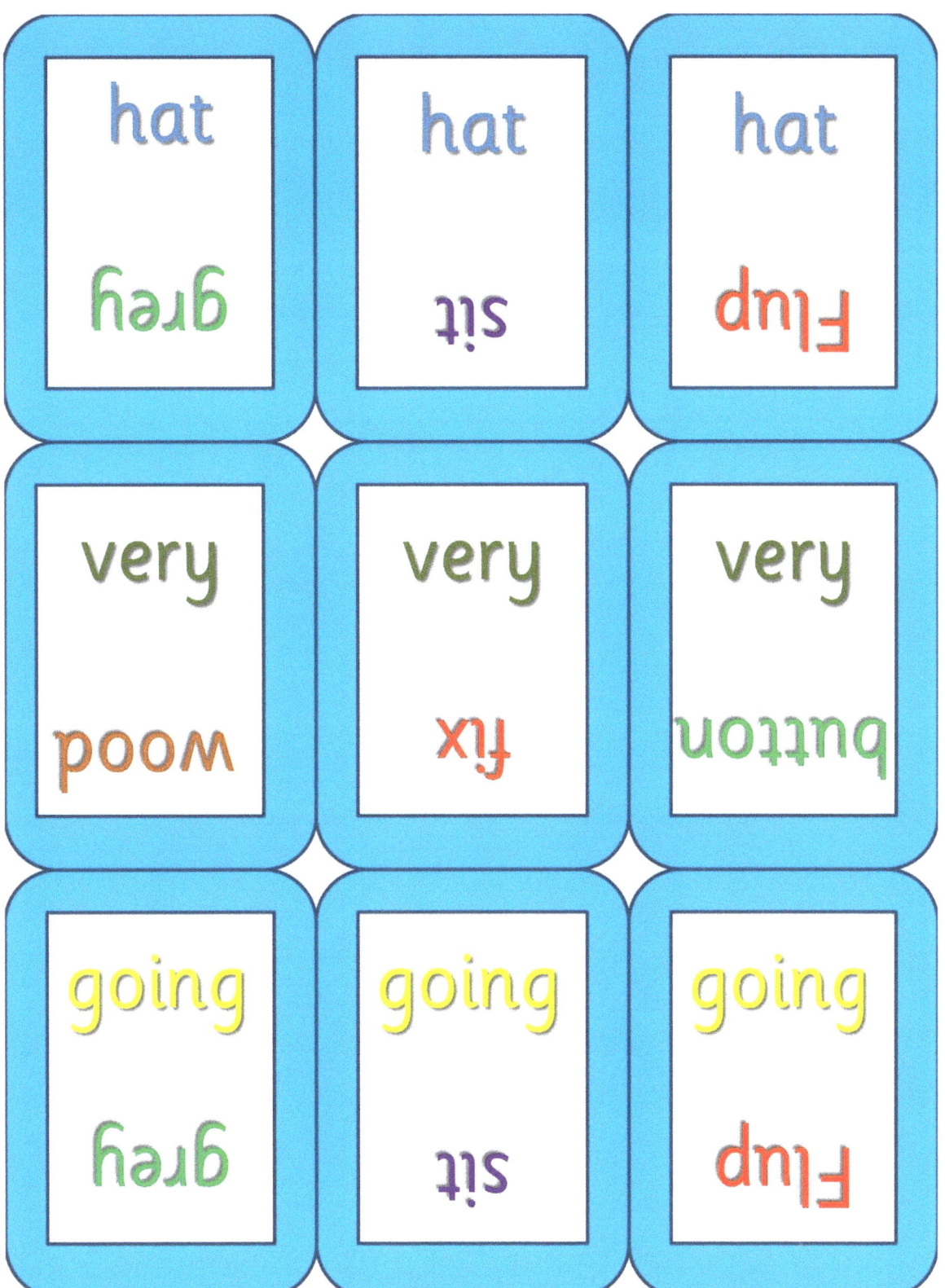

Book 7 Dominoes sheet 3

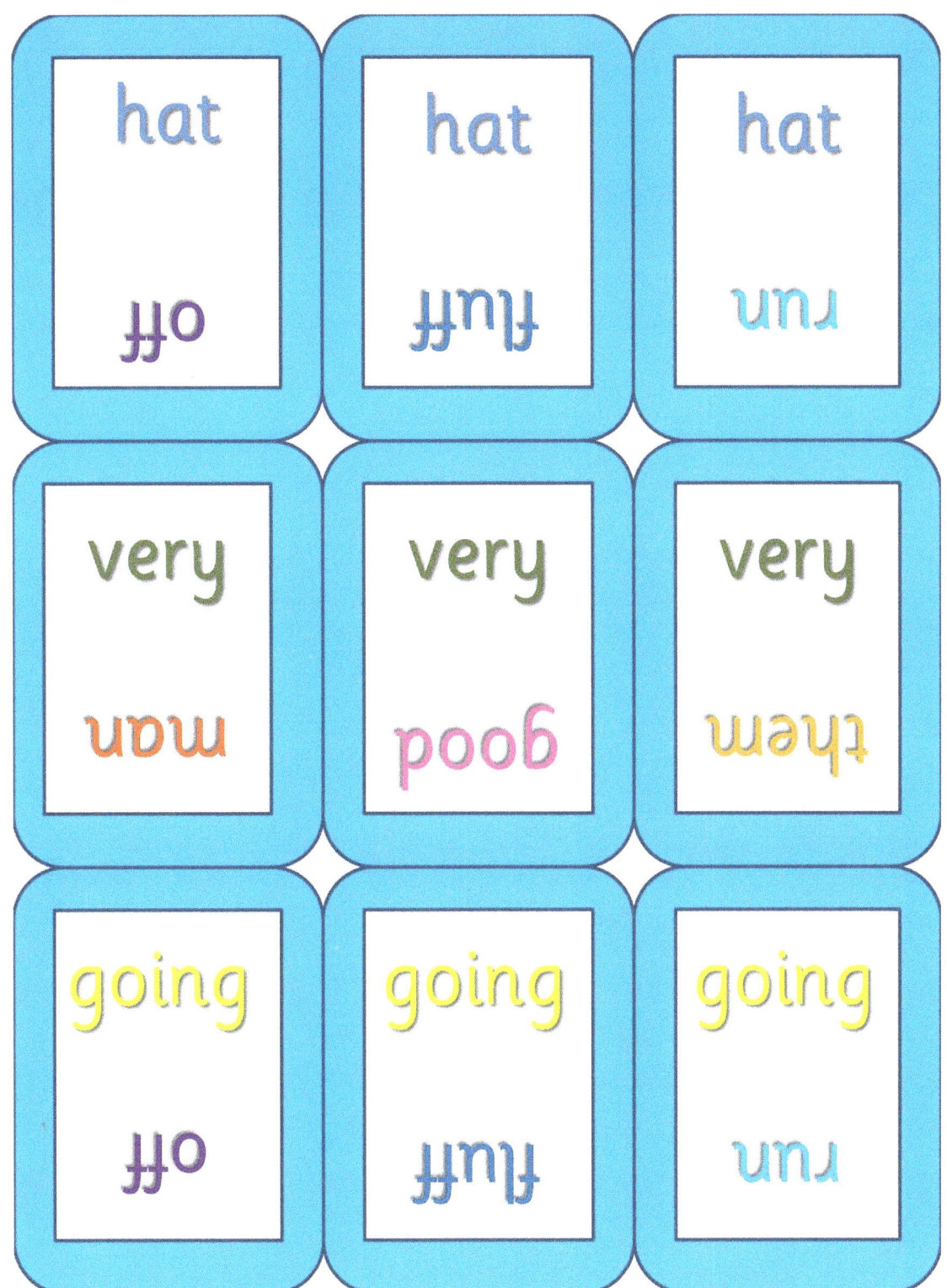

Book 7 Dominoes sheet 4

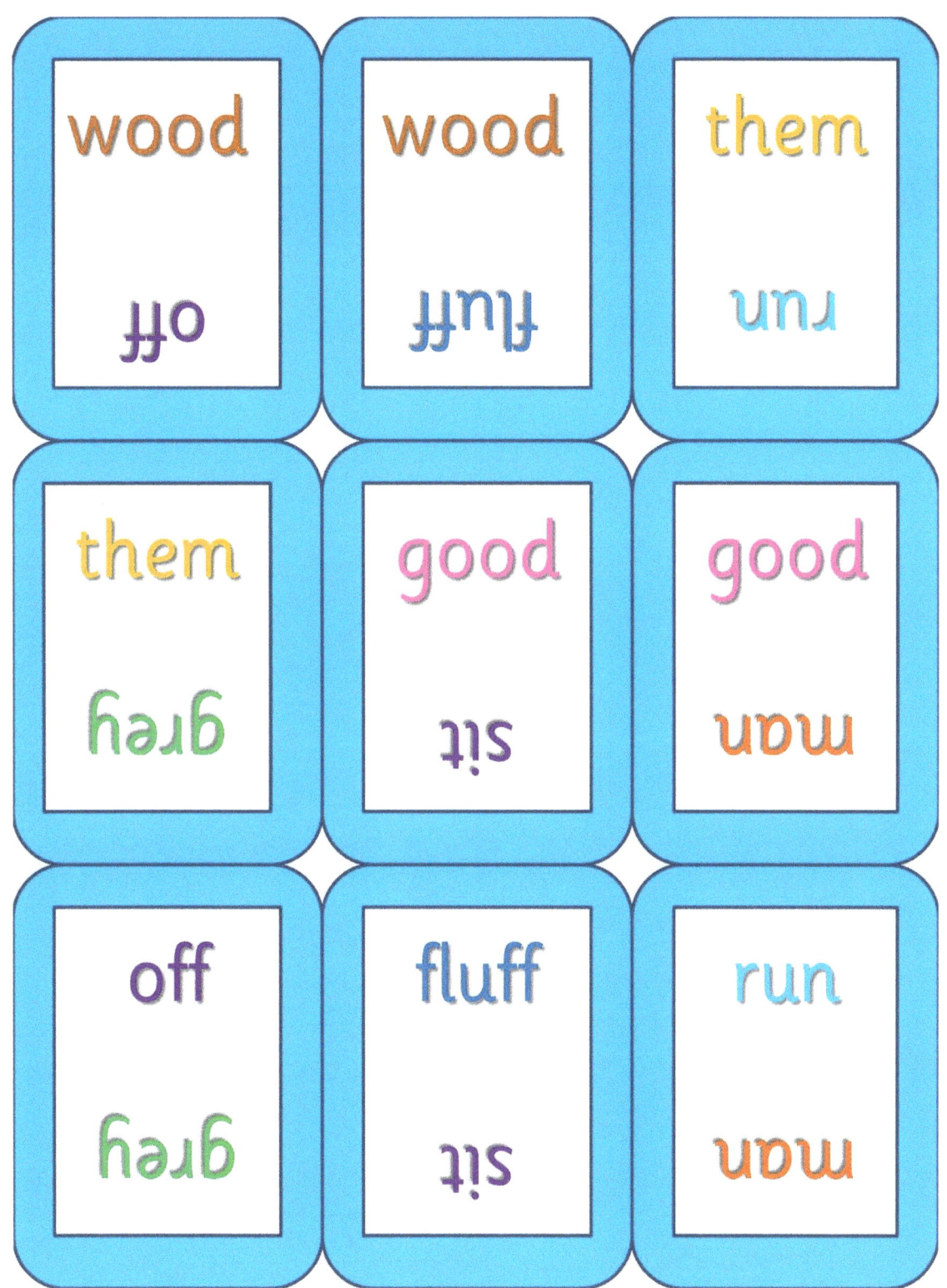

Book 7 Dominoes sheet 5

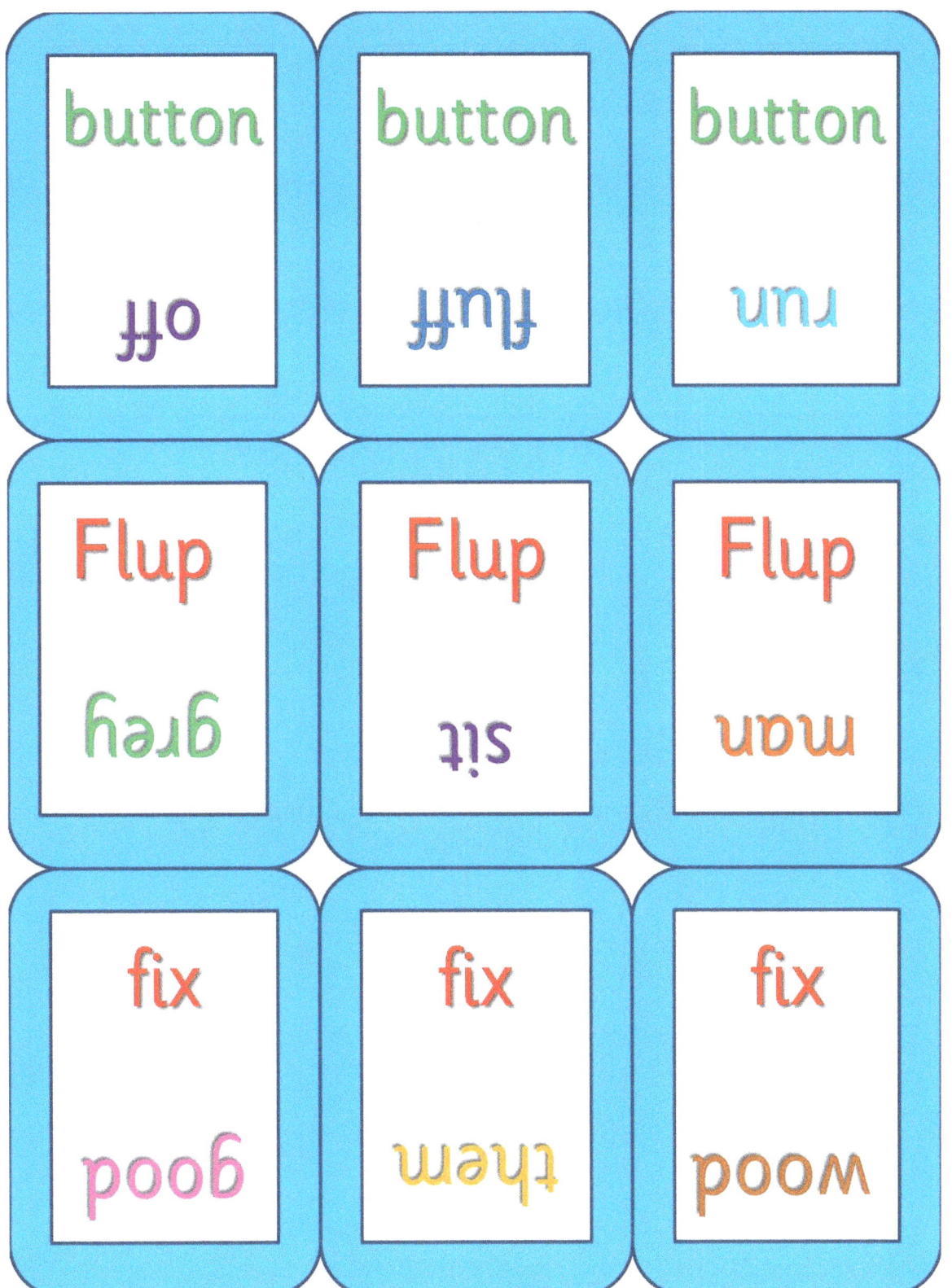

Book 7 Dominoes sheet 6

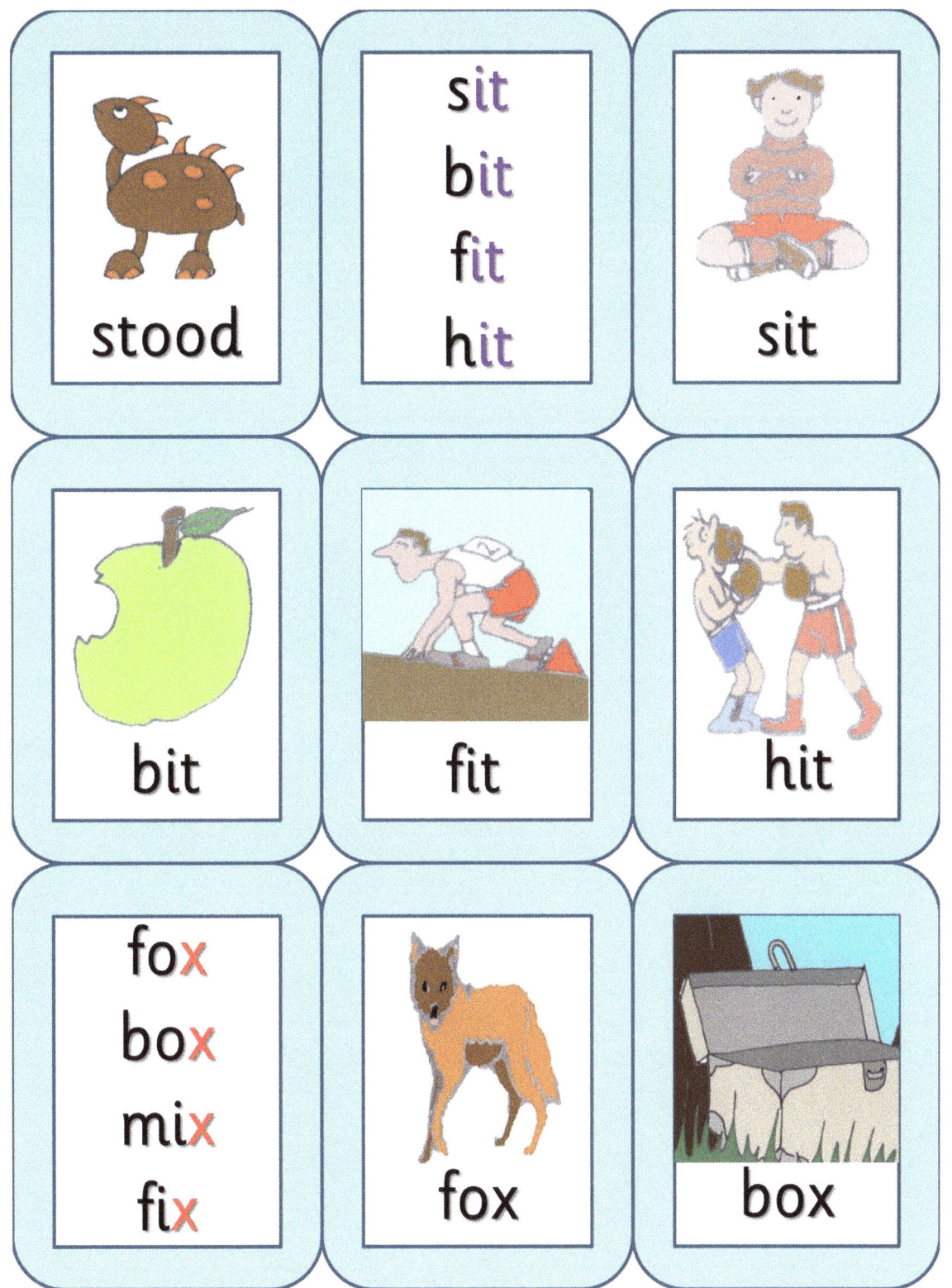

Book 7 Happy Word Families sheet 2

Happy Word Families (for 4 players)

- Give each player a master card (with a list of words)

- These cards are placed face up in front of the player

- The remaining cards are shuffled and shared out equally

- Players take turns clockwise to ask another player if they have a card from their family

- If they have the requested card they must hand it over

- If they do not have the requested card, it is the next player's turn

- The winner is the first to collect the whole of their family

Book 7 Happy Word Families sheet 3

Cut along bold lines and feed through the window

hat	so	sit	man	very
going	run	off	box	grey
button	tell	them	bit	good
Flup	bed	wood	fix	fluff

Book 7 Octologo word sheet
Print 1 for each player

Saff 8

Word list:

twig	all	puff	band	stay
bees	they	hit	stuff	huff
Saff	spy	bang	hang	clang
black	to	be	sang	way

Targeted phonics:

_ang
_uff
_nk
tw_
th_

High frequency words:

all
they
to
be

Text:
1. The tall tree by the pond.
2. A twig on the tree.
3. An old nest for bees.
4. This weebee is Saff. She has black wings.
5. She can fly in the sky with Jig.
6. Saff, Jig and Flup can all fly. They spy Mop and Tod by the wall.
7. Mop is going to sing. Tod wil puff into the old shell.
8. Saff can hit the metal box. She can bang it with her black wings.
9. They can all be a band.
10. Tod will get stuff from the wood.
11. Flup can hang this for Jig to bang.
12. The band is good. Mop sang a good song.
13. They will stay and play a long song.
14. Tod will huff and puff. Saff will bang and clang. Grog is on his way to see the band.

Book 8 Fishing Lotto card 1

Book 8 fish for card 1

Attach either brass butterfly clips or simply use a staple for fishing with a magnet.

Book 8 fish for card 2

Attach either brass butterfly clips or simply use a staple for fishing with a magnet.

Book 8 Memory game sheet 1

Book 8 Memory game sheet 2

Book 8 Happy Word Families sheet 2

Happy Word Families (for 4 players)

- Give each player a master card (with a list of words)

- These cards are placed face up in front of the player

- The remaining cards are shuffled and shared out equally

- Players take turns clockwise to ask another player if they have a card from their family

- If they have the requested card they must hand it over

- If they do not have the requested card, it is the next player's turn

- The winner is the first to collect the whole of their family

Book 8 Happy Word Families sheet 3

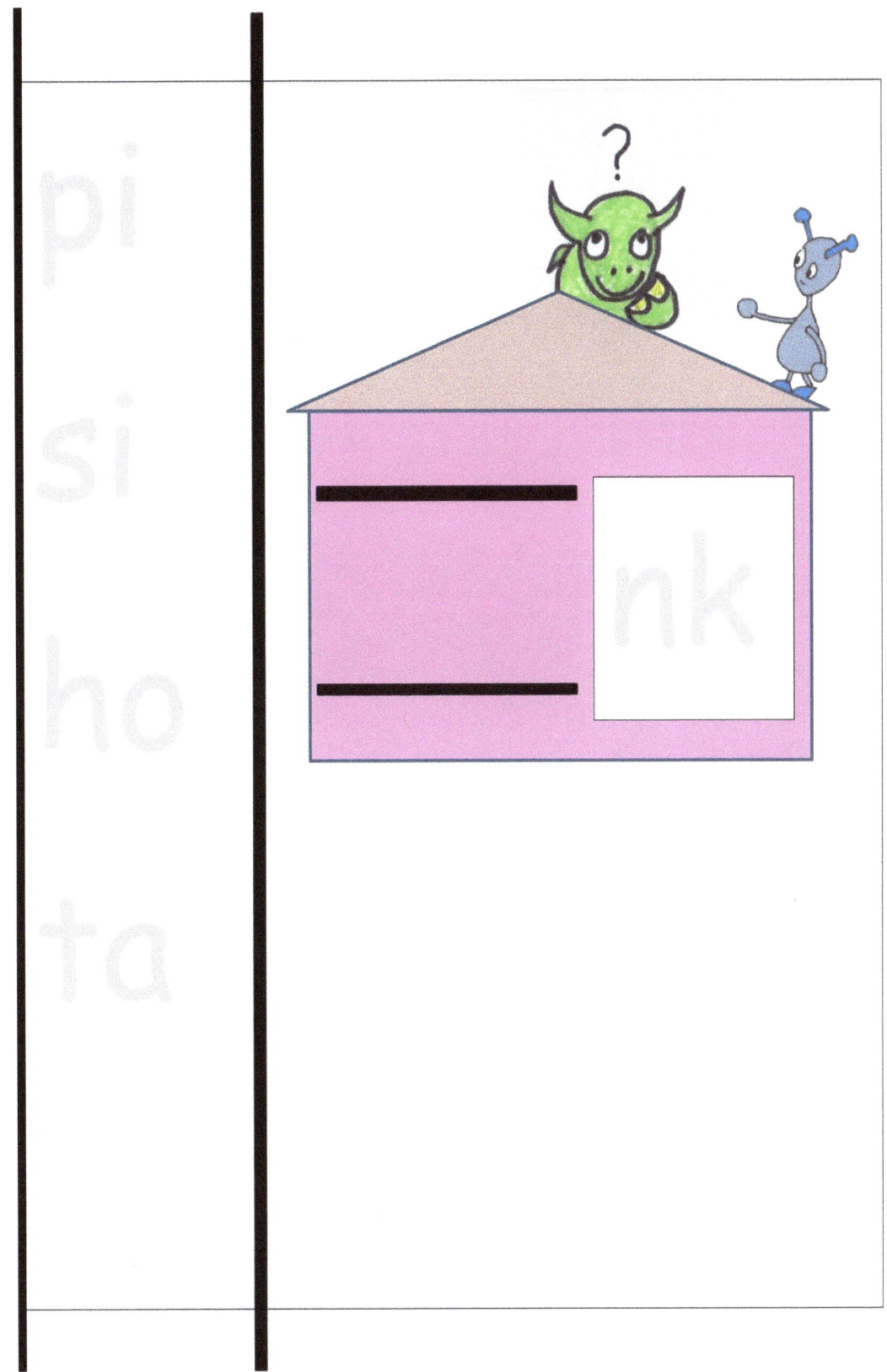

Cut along bold lines and feed through the window

stay	band	puff	all	twig
huff	stuff	hit	they	bees
clang	hang	bang	spy	Saff
way	sang	be	to	black

Book 8 Octologo word sheet
Print 1 for each player

Pupil Tracker				
Name:			
Book	Activity	Date of 1st occurrence	Date of 2nd occurrence
1	Bingo		
	Dominoes		
	Phonics sheet		
2	Fishing Lotto		
	Memory		
	Phonics sheet		
3	Bingo		
	Dominoes		
	Phonics sheet		
	Octologo		
4	Fishing Lotto		
	Memory		
	Happy Word Families		
	Phonics sheet		
	Octologo		
5	Bingo		
	Dominoes		
	Happy Word Families		
	Phonics sheet		
	Octologo		
6	Fishing Lotto		
	Memory		
	Happy Word Families		
	Phonics sheet		
	Octologo		
7	Bingo		
	Dominoes		
	Happy Word Families		
	Phonics sheet		
	Octologo		
8	Fishing Lotto		
	Memory		
	Happy Word Families		
	Phonics sheet		
	Octologo		

www.ingramcontent.com/pod-product-compliance
Lightning Source LLC
Chambersburg PA
CBHW040927240426
43667CB00024B/2975